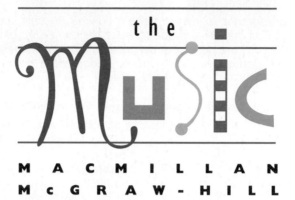

SHARE the Music

MACMILLAN McGRAW-HILL

AUTHORS

Judy Bond,
Coordinating Author
René Boyer-White
Margaret Campbelle-duGard
Marilyn Copeland Davidson,
Coordinating Author
Robert de Frece
Mary Goetze,
Coordinating Author
Doug Goodkin
Betsy M. Henderson

Michael Jothen
Carol King
Vincent P. Lawrence,
Coordinating Author
Nancy L. T. Miller
Ivy Rawlins
Susan Snyder,
Coordinating Author

Janet McMillion,
Contributing Writer

Macmillan/McGraw-Hill School Publishing Company
New York • Columbus

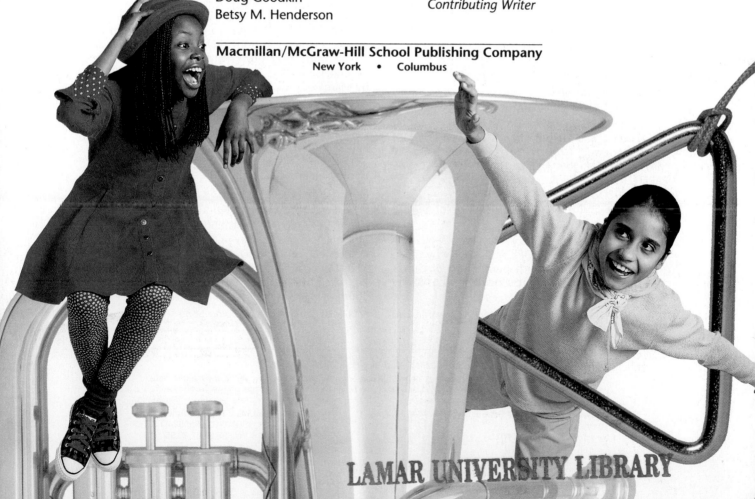

ACKNOWLEDGMENTS

Grateful acknowledgment is given to the following authors, composers, and publishers. Every effort has been made to trace the ownership of all copyrighted material and to secure the necessary permissions to reprint these selections. In the case of some selections for which acknowledgment is not given, extensive research has failed to locate the copyright holders.

ACUM Ltd. for *Hag Asif* by Sarah Levy-Tanai and Moshe Rappaport. Copyright © Levy-Tanai & Rappaport Moshe, Israel. English lyrics © Laura Koulish.

Fran Smartt Addicott for *The Delta Queen* by Fran Smartt Addicott. Copyright © Fran Smartt Addicott.

Alfred Publishing Co., Inc. for *Yuki (Snow)* from FAVORITE SONGS OF JAPANESE CHILDREN, translated and collected by Hanako Fukuda. Copyright © MCMLXV by Highland Music Co. Copyright © assigned MCMXC to Alfred Publishing Co., Inc. Used by Permission of the Publisher.

Appalsongs Productions for *The Kindergarten Wall* by John McCutcheon from MAIL MYSELF TO YOU (Rounder 8016). Copyright © 1988 by John McCutcheon/Appalsongs (ASCAP).

Boosey & Hawkes, Inc. for *Gavotta* from SYMPHONIE CLASSIQUE by Sergei Prokofiev. © 1926 by Edition Russe de Musique. Copyright assigned to Boosey & Hawkes Inc., for the world. Reprinted by permission. For *The Piglet's Christmas* (Mary Goetze/Nancy Cooper). Copyright © 1988 by Boosey & Hawkes, Inc. This arrangement is made with the permission of Boosey & Hawkes, Inc. Reprinted by permission.

Butterside Music for *I'll Rise When the Rooster Crows*, lyrics by David Holt. Copyright © 1983 Butterside Music, P.O. Box 8843, Asheville, NC 28814.

W. Jay Cawley for *All Living Things* by W. Jay Cawley. Copyright © 1992 W. Jay Cawley.

CPP/Belwin, Inc. for *We're Off to See the Wizard* by E.Y. Harburg and Harold Arlen. Copyright © 1938, 1939 (Renewed 1966, 1967) METRO-GOLDWYN MAYER, INC., Rights Assigned to EMI CATALOGUE PARTNERSHIP. All Rights Controlled & Administered by EMI FEIST CATALOGUE, INC. International Copyright Secured. Made in USA. All Rights Reserved.

Curtis Brown Group Ltd. for *They Were My People* from COME INTO MY TROPICAL GARDEN by Grace Nichols. Reproduced with permission of Curtis Brown Group Ltd., London. Copyright © 1988 by Grace Nichols.

Emma Lou Diemer for *Seven Limericks* by Emma Lou Diemer. Copyright © 1967 by Emma Lou Diemer.

Ell-Bern Publishing Company for *Jambo*, words and music by Ella Jenkins, Ell-Bern Publishing Company, ASCAP.

Geordie Music Publishing Co. for *Killy Kranky* by Jean Ritchie. Copyright © 1955, 1965 Jean Richie, Geordie Music Publishing Co.

Grossett & Dunlap for *Ema Ma* from OUT OF THE EARTH I SING: POETRY AND SONGS OF PRIMITIVE PEOPLES OF THE WORLD. Copyright © 1968 by Richard Lewis. Used by permission of Grosset & Dunlap.

Harcourt Brace Jovanovich, Inc. for *Dance of the Animals* from THE AFRICAN SAGA by Blaise Cendrars, reprinted by permission of Harcourt Brace Jovanovich, Inc.

HarperCollins Publishers, Inc. for *Clink, an iced branch falls* by Kazue Mizumura from FLOWER MOON SNOW: A BOOK OF HAIKU by Kazue Mizumura. Copyright © by Kazue Mizumura. For *Music* from ELEANOR FARJEON'S POEMS FOR CHILDREN by Eleanor Farjeon. *Music* originally appeared in SING FOR YOUR SUPPER by Eleanor Farjeon. Copyright 1938 by Eleanor Farjeon. Renewed 1966 by Gervase Farjeon. For *Rope Rhyme* by Eloise Greenfield from HONEY, I LOVE by Eloise Greenfield. Text copyright © 1978 by Eloise Greenfield. For *The Secret Song* from NIBBLE NIBBLE by Margaret Wise Brown. Text copyright © 1959 by William R. Scott, Inc. Renewed 1987 by Roberta Brown Rauch.

Henry Holt and Company for *Mabel, Mabel* from ROCKET IN MY POCKET by Carl Withers. Copyright © 1948 by Carl Withers. Reprinted by permission of Henry Holt and Co., Inc.

Fidelia Jimerson for *Seneca Stomp Dance* by Avery Jimerson. Used by permission.

Memphis Musicraft Publications for *Halloween Night* by Doris Parker and *They're Out of Sight* by Michael D. Bennett from HOLIDAYS–21 FESTIVE ARRANGE-MENTS, Copyright © 1980 Michael D. Bennett. Published by Memphis Musicraft Publications, 3149 Southern Ave., Memphis, TN 38111.

MGA for *Rattlesnake Skipping Song* by Dennis Lee,

continued on page 389

Macmillan/McGraw-Hill School Division
10 Union Square East
New York, New York 10003

Printed in the United States of America
ISBN 0-02-295052-4 / 3
3 4 5 6 7 8 9 VHJ 99 98 97 96 95

SPECIAL CONTRIBUTORS

Contributing Writer
Janet McMillion

Consultant Writers
Teri Burdette, Signing
Brian Burnett, Movement
Robert Duke, Assessment
Joan Gregoryk, Vocal Development/ Choral
Judith Jellison, Special Learners/ Assessment
Jacque Schrader, Movement
Kathy B. Sorensen, International Phonetic Alphabet
Mollie Tower, Listening

Consultants
Lisa DeLorenzo, Critical Thinking
Nancy Ferguson, Jazz/Improvisation
Judith Nayer, Poetry
Marta Sanchez, Dalcroze
Mollie Tower, Reviewer
Robyn Turner, Fine Arts

Multicultural Consultants
Judith Cook Tucker
JaFran Jones
Oscar Muñoz
Marta Sanchez
Edwin J. Schupman, Jr., of ORBIS Associates
Mary Shamrock
Kathy B. Sorensen

Multicultural Advisors
Shailaja Akkapeddi (Hindi), Edna Alba (Ladino), Gregory Amobi (Ibu), Thomas Appiah (Ga, Twi, Fanti), Deven Asay (Russian), Vera Auman (Russian, Ukrainian), David Azman (Hebrew), Lissa Bangeter (Portuguese), Britt Marie Barnes (Swedish), Dr. Mark Bell (French), Brad Ahawanrathe Bonaparte (Mohawk), Chhanda Chakroborti (Hindi), Ninthalangsonk Chanthasen (Laotian), Julius Chavez (Navajo), Lin-Rong Chen (Mandarin), Anna Cheng (Mandarin), Rushen Chi (Mandarin), T. L. Chi (Mandarin), Michelle Chingwa (Ottowa), Hoon Choi (Korean), James Comarell (Greek), Lynn DePaula (Portuguese), Ketan Dholakia (Gujarati), Richard O. Effiong (Nigerian), Nayereh Fallahi (Persian), Angela Fields (Hopi, Chemehuevi), Gary Fields (Lakota, Cree), Siri Veslemoy Fluge (Norwegian), Katalin Forrai (Hungarian), Renee Galagos (Swedish), Linda Goodman, Judith A. Gray, Savyasachi Gupta (Marati), Elizabeth Haile (Shinnecock), Mary Harouny (Persian), Charlotte Heth (Cherokee), Tim Hunt (Vietnamese), Marcela Janko (Czech), Raili Jeffrey (Finnish), Rita Jensen (Danish), Teddy Kaiahura (Swahili), Gueen Kalaw (Tagalog), Merehau Kamai (Tahitian), Richard Keeling, Masanori Kimura (Japanese), Chikahide Komura (Japanese), Saul Korewa (Hebrew), Jagadishwar Kota (Tamil), Sokun Koy (Cambodian), Craig Kurumada (Balkan), Cindy Trong Le (Vietnamese), Dongchoon Lee (Korean), Young-Jing Lee (Korean), Nomi Lob (Hebrew), Sam Loeng (Mandarin, Malay), Georgia Magpie (Comanche), Mladen Marič (Croatian), Kuinise Matagi (Samoan), Hiromi Matsushita (Japanese), Jackie Maynard (Hawaiian), David McAllester, Mike Kanathohare McDonald (Mohawk), Khumbulani Mdlefshe (Zulu), Martin Mkize (Xhosa), David Montgomery (Turkish), Kazadi Big Musungayi (Swahili), Professor Akiya Nakamara (Japanese), Edwin Napia (Maori), Hang Nguyen (Vietnamese), Richard Nielsen (Danish), Wil Numkena (Hopi), Eva Ochoa (Spanish), Drora Oren (Hebrew), Jackie Osherow (Yiddish), Mavis Oswald (Russian), Dr. Dil Parkinson (Arabic), Kenny Tahawisoren Perkins (Mohawk), Alvin Petersen (Sotho), Phay Phan (Cambodian), Charlie Phim (Cambodian), Aroha Price (Maori), Marg Puiri (Samoan), John Rainer (Taos Pueblo, Creek), Lillian Rainer (Taos Pueblo, Creek, Apache), Winton Ria (Maori), Arnold Richardson (Haliwa-Saponi), Thea Roscher (German), Dr. Wayne Sabey (Japanese), Regine Saintil (Bamboula Creole), Luci Scherzer (German), Ken Sekaquaptewa (Hopi), Samouen Seng (Cambodian), Pei Shin (Mandarin), Dr. Larry Shumway (Japanese), Gwen Shunatona (Pawnee, Otoe, Potawatomi), Ernest Siva (Cahuilla, Serrano [Maringa´]), Ben Snowball (Inuit), Dr. Michelle Stott (German), Keiko Tanefuji (Japanese), James Taylor (Portuguese), Shiu-wai Tong (Mandarin), Tom Toronto (Lao, Thai), Lynn Tran (Vietnamese), Gulavadee Vaz (Thai), Chen Ying Wang (Taiwanese), Masakazu Watabe (Japanese), Freddy Wheeler (Navajo), Keith Yackeyonny (Comanche), Liming Yang (Mandarin), Edgar Zurita (Andean)

CONTENTS

v

GAMES WE SHARE

Rope Rhyme

Get set, ready now, jump right in
Bounce and kick and giggle and spin
Listen to the rope when it hits the ground
Listen to the clappedy-slappedy sound
Jump right up when it tells you to
Come back down, whatever you do
Count to a hundred, count by ten
Start to count all over again
That's what jumping is all about
Get set, ready now
jump
right
out!

—Eloise Greenfield

1

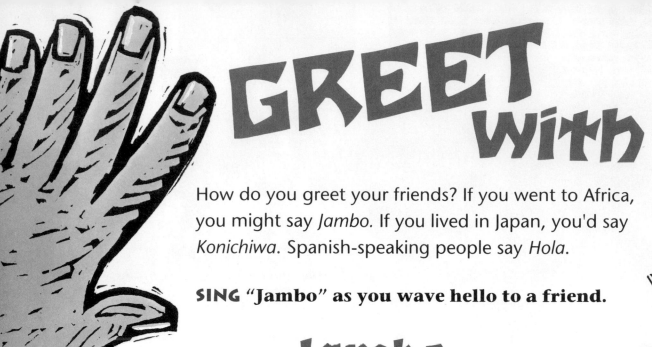

GREET With a

How do you greet your friends? If you went to Africa, you might say *Jambo.* If you lived in Japan, you'd say *Konichiwa.* Spanish-speaking people say *Hola.*

SING "Jambo" as you wave hello to a friend.

Jambo
Hello

Words and Music
by Ella Jenkins

Call
Bm   *Response*

do

Swahili:	**Jam**	**bo,** _____			jam	bo, _____
Pronunciation:	jam	bo			jam	bo
English:	**Hel**	**lo,** _____			hel	lo, _____

Call
Em   Bm

Jam - bo sa - na,   jam - bo. _____
jam   bo   sa   na   jam   bo
hel-lo ev'-ry - bod - y   hel - lo. _____

Response
Em   Bm

Jam - bo sa - na,   jam - bo. _____
jam   bo   sa   na   jam   bo
Hel-lo, ev'-ry - bod - y   hel - lo. _____

Spanish

2. **Hola, hola, hola mis amigos, hola.**
o la o la o la mis a mi gos o la
Hola, mis amigos, hola.
o la mis a mi gos o la

Japanese

3. おはようおはようおはようこんにちはおはよう
o ha yo o ha yo o ha yo kon ni chi wa o ha yo
おはようこんにちはおはよう
o ha yo kon ni chi wa o ha yo

BEAT

Children in Cleveland, Ohio, made up this funny rhyme. They used the **rhythm of the words** to make the rhyme into a **speech piece**.

LISTEN to the speech piece "Bonefish, Bluebird" and tap each bar with the *steady beat*.

Bonefish, Bluebird

Speech piece by Ruth Hamm and
Isabel McNeill Carley
Words Adapted by MMH

Bone-	fish,	blue-	bird,	sheep	and	flea,	
Chick-a-	dee,	doo-dle	bug,	rob-ins	in	a	tree.
Fly	in	the	cream	jar.	Frog	in	the	pool.
Clap for	all	the	chil-	dren	here	at	school.

FIND the beat of silence in each line.

COMPARE the beat with the rhythm of the words. How are they different?

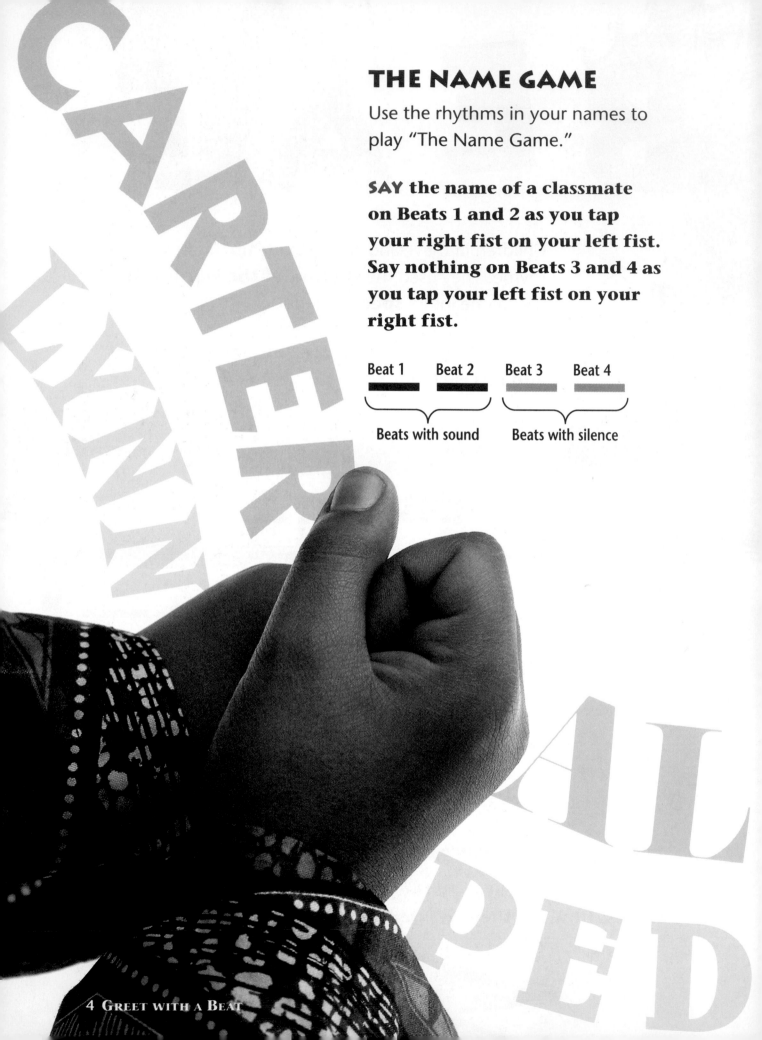

THE NAME GAME

Use the rhythms in your names to play "The Name Game."

SAY the name of a classmate on Beats 1 and 2 as you tap your right fist on your left fist. Say nothing on Beats 3 and 4 as you tap your left fist on your right fist.

Beat 1   Beat 2   Beat 3   Beat 4

Beats with sound   Beats with silence

PLAYING WITH PATTERNS

Children in Ghana, a country in Africa, use rhythms to play a stone-passing game. You can learn the rhythms and the game, too!

PAT on Beats 1 and 2. Make no sound on Beats 3 and 4.

Which beats have sound? Which beats have silence? This four-beat pattern is called a **rhythm pattern** because it repeats.

Pat left
Beat 1

Pat right
Beat 2

Thumbs
Beat 3

Thumbs
Beat 4

You can use the four-beat rhythm pattern with "Ɔboɔ Asi Me Nsa," a song from Africa. The pattern will help you to play the stone-passing game.

LISTEN to "Ɔboɔ Asi Me Nsa" as you pat the four-beat rhythm pattern.

Ɔboɔ Asi Me Nsa

Akan Stone-Passing Game

Freely

Akan: Ɔ boɔ asi me nsa na - na Ɔ-boɔ asi me nsa,

Pronunciation: ɔ boɔ si mɛn sa na na ɔ boɔ si mɛn sa

Ɔ-boɔ asi me nsa na - na Ɔ-boɔ asi me nsa.

ɔ boɔ si mɛn sa na na ɔ boɔ si mɛn sa

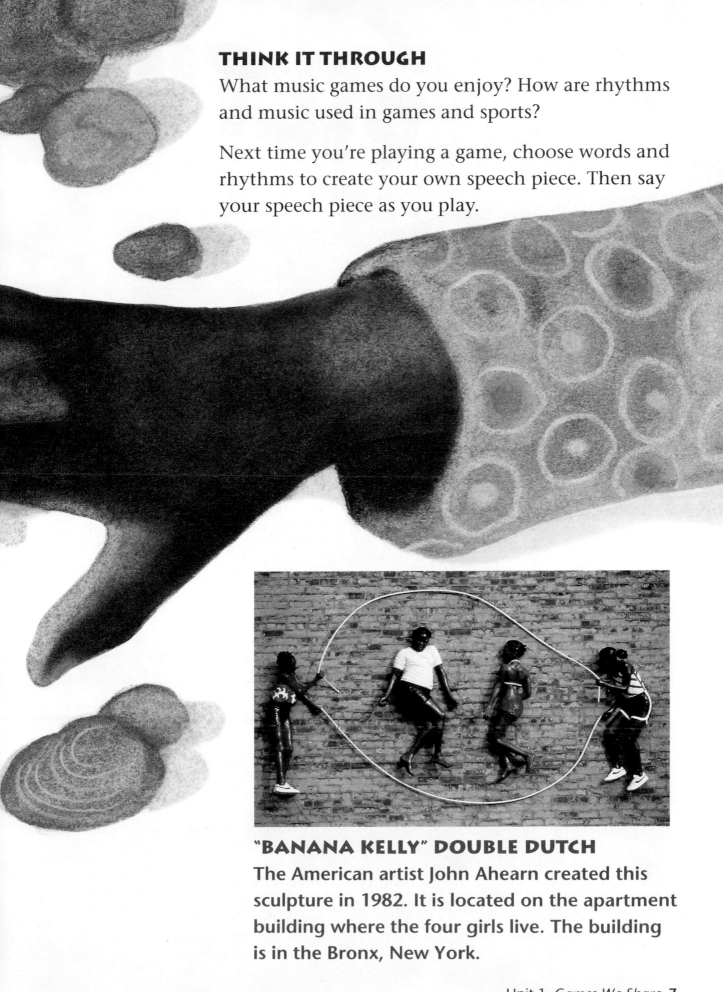

THINK IT THROUGH

What music games do you enjoy? How are rhythms and music used in games and sports?

Next time you're playing a game, choose words and rhythms to create your own speech piece. Then say your speech piece as you play.

"BANANA KELLY" DOUBLE DUTCH

The American artist John Ahearn created this sculpture in 1982. It is located on the apartment building where the four girls live. The building is in the Bronx, New York.

A mountain range has high peaks and low valleys. When you sing, your voice makes high and low sounds, or **pitches**. A line of pitches that moves up, down, or repeats is called a **melody**.

LISTEN to "Rocky Mountain" as you trace the shape of the melody below.

Appalachian Folk Song

ROCKY MOUNTAIN

tain high,

moun-

tain,   tain,

Rock-y moun-   rock-y moun-   rock-y

8

A Melody

When you're on that rock-y moun-tain, hang your head and cry.

Refrain:
Do, do, do, do, Do remember me.
Do, do, do, do, Do remember me.

2. Sunny valley, sunny valley,
   sunny valley, low,
   When you're in that sunny
   valley, sing it soft and slow.
   Refrain

3. Stormy ocean, stormy ocean,
   stormy ocean wide,
   When you're in that deep
   blue sea, there's no place
   you can hide.
   Refrain

DANCE A STORY

Songs like "Rocky Mountain" tell stories with words and music. A **ballet** tells a story using dance and music.

LISTENING

Sabre Dance
by Aram Khachaturian

The ballet Gayane *tells about men who try to steal from some farmers.*

The farmers find out about the robbers and catch them. Because the farmers are happy, they dance the "Sabre Dance."

TRACE the shape of the "Sabre Dance" melody. Does the melody move mainly up, down, or with repeated pitches?

INTRODUCTION
16 beats

Ⓐ MAIN THEME

a   a   a'   a'

Ⓑ

① ② ③ ④

flute second time

BRIDGE

△A' a   a'   a'

CODA

Here's a chance for you to find "peaks" and "valleys" in another melody.

LISTEN to "Long-Legged Sailor" and trace the shape of the melody.

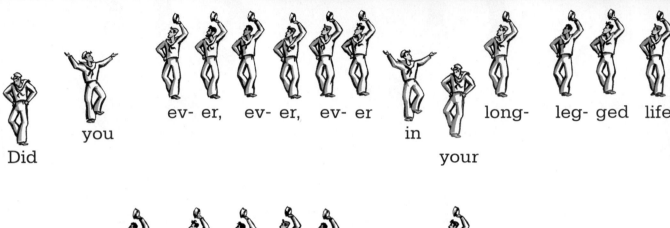

Did you ev- er, ev- er, ev- er in your long- leg- ged life

Meet a long- leg- ged sail- or with a long- leg- ged wife?

FIND words in a row that repeat.

Does the melody move up, down, or repeat on those words?

THINK IT THROUGH

Compare the shape of this melody with the "Sabre Dance" theme. How are they alike?

LONG-LEGGED SAILOR

Game Chant

1.-5. Did you ev - er, ev - er, ev - er in your
{ long - leg - ged
short - leg - ged
knock-kneed ——
bow - leg - ged
cross - leg - ged } life

Meet a long - leg-ged* sail - or with a long - leg-ged* wife?

No I nev - er, nev - er, nev - er in my
{ long - leg - ged
short - leg - ged
knock-kneed ——
bow - leg - ged
cross - leg - ged } life

Met a long - leg-ged* sail - or with a long - leg-ged* wife.

* *change word for verses 2-5*

The Color of Your Voice

You have your very own fingerprint.

You also have your own voice print. A voice print of your singing might look like this.

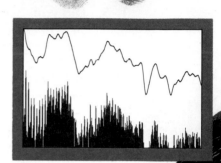

A voice print of a friend's singing might look like this.

The special sound of your voice is called its **tone color**.

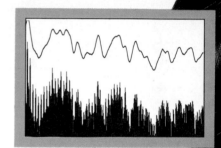

SAME VOICE, DIFFERENT TONE COLORS

You can make heavier and lighter sounds with your voice. This picture shows a person singing a pitch in a **heavier voice**.

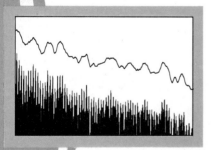

This picture shows the same person singing the same pitch in a **lighter voice**.

LISTEN to "Bonefish, Bluebird" in a heavier voice and then in a lighter voice.

CHOOSE your heavier or lighter voice and say "Bonefish, Bluebird."

THINK IT THROUGH

How does saying "Bonefish, Bluebird" in a heavier or lighter voice change its feeling?

SINGING WITH TWO VOICES

Just as you can speak in a heavier or lighter voice, you can sing in a heavier or lighter voice. Listen to "Down by the River" sung both ways.

CHOOSE your heavier or lighter voice to sing this song.

Down by the River

African American Singing Game

1. Down by the river two by two, two by two, two by two.
   Down by the river two by two, now rise Sally rise.

2. Let me see you make a motion two by two, . . .

3. Now take another partner two by two, . . .

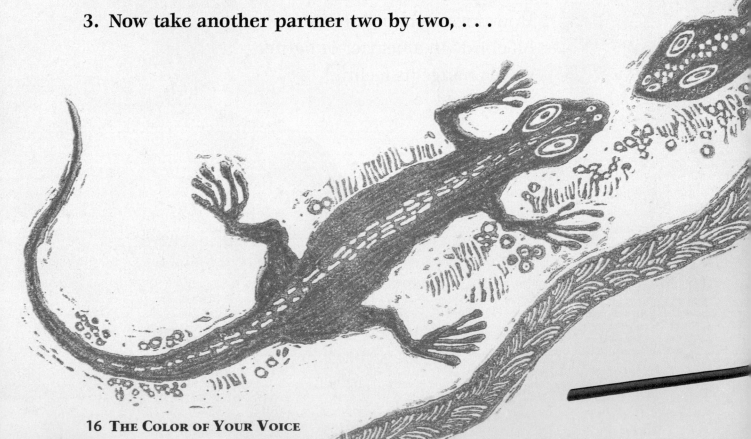

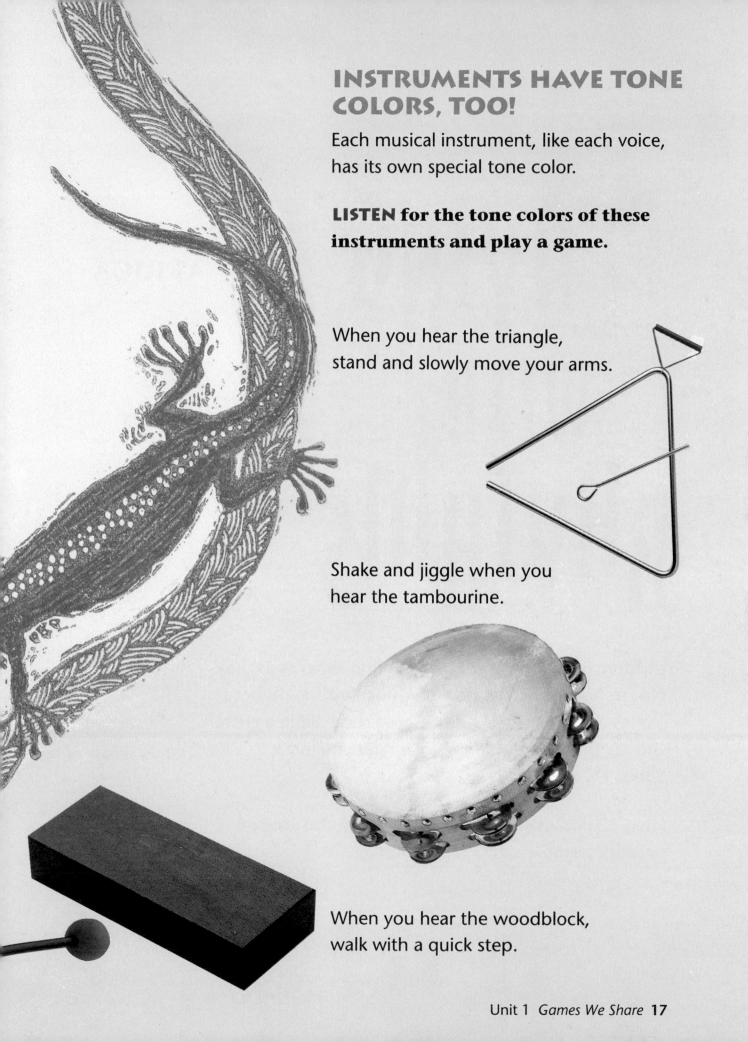

INSTRUMENTS HAVE TONE COLORS, TOO!

Each musical instrument, like each voice, has its own special tone color.

LISTEN for the tone colors of these instruments and play a game.

When you hear the triangle, stand and slowly move your arms.

Shake and jiggle when you hear the tambourine.

When you hear the woodblock, walk with a quick step.

PLAYING WITH RHYTHMS

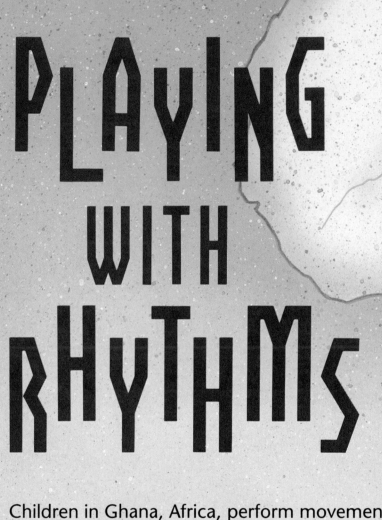

AFRICA

Ghana

Children in Ghana, Africa, perform movements as they play stone-passing games. You can enjoy one of these games with the song "Ɔboɔ Asi Me Nsa." Sit in a circle and say *grab, pass, thumbs, thumbs* as you listen to "Ɔboɔ Asi Me Nsa."

SING "Ɔboɔ Asi Me Nsa" as you play the stone-passing game.

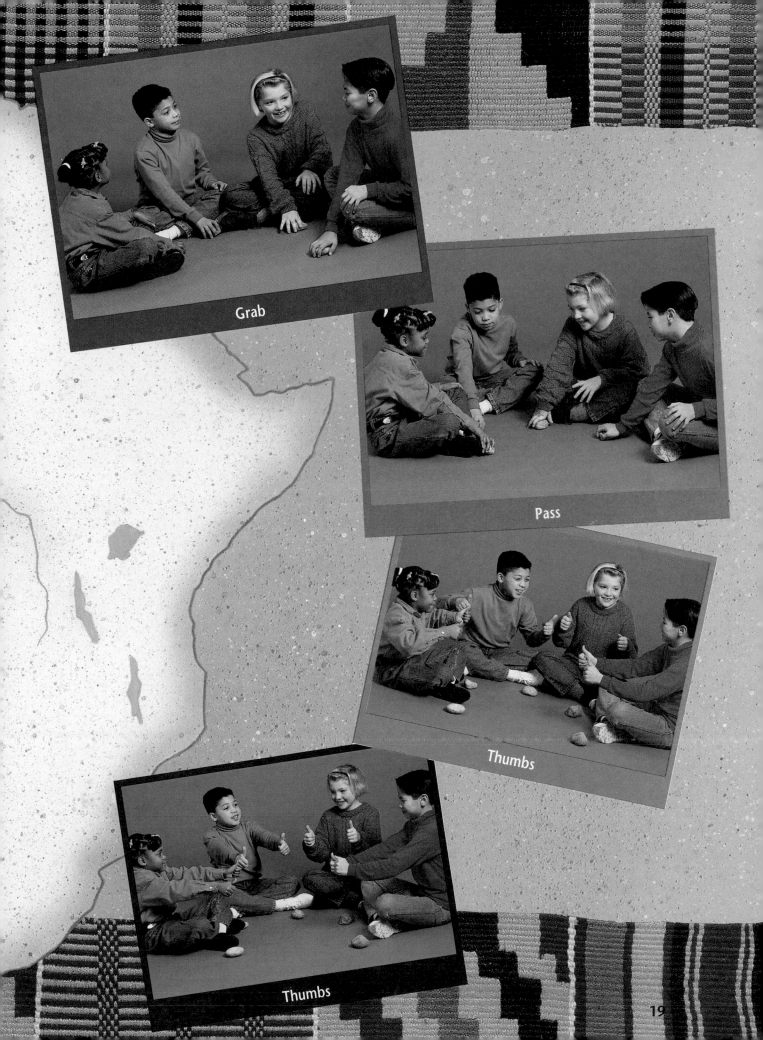

Grab

Pass

Thumbs

Thumbs

ROCKY MOUNTAIN RHYTHMS

The rhythm of "Rocky Mountain" has one sound, two sounds, and no sound to a beat.

quarter note
(one sound)

eighth notes
(two sounds)

quarter rest
(no sound)

CLAP the rhythm of "Rocky Mountain"
as you say the words.

Rock - y   moun-tain, rock - y   moun-tain, rock - y   moun-tain high,

The **meter signature** ² of "Rocky Mountain"
tells you that the beats are felt in sets of two. Each set
of two beats is called a **measure. Bar lines** separate
the measures.

CLAP this rhythm as you say *rock* for ♩ and
moun-tain for ♫

How many measures are in this rhythm?

*"Rocky Mountain" was first sung by people who lived near the
Appalachian Mountains. This area is a center for the folk arts,
such as making dolls, baskets, quilts, and dulcimers.*

A "SURPRISING" RHYTHM!

The rhythms in "Rocky Mountain" can be found in much of the music you sing, play, or listen to.

READ these rhythms, saying *tip-toe* for 🎵 and *look* for ♩

1.

2.

LISTENING

"Surprise" Symphony
No. 94, Second Movement (excerpt)
by Franz Joseph Haydn

LISTENING MAP *Tap on the pictures in this listening map as you listen to the "Surprise" Symphony.*

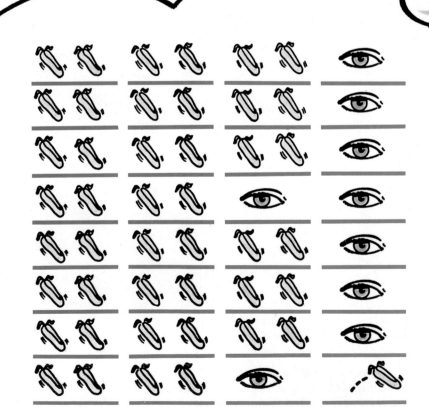

MOVE as you listen to the "Surprise" Symphony again. Say the words *tip-toe* and *look* as you move. On the last note say *jump*, and make the largest shape you can.

Which of these rhythms is repeated in the first part of the "Surprise" Symphony? Which of these rhythms has the "Surprise" in it?

Spotlight on

Franz Joseph Haydn

Franz Joseph Haydn (1732–1809) was an Austrian composer who wrote the "Surprise" Symphony for a special after-dinner concert. He knew that many of the people might be using this concert as their nap time, so he used calm string music. He gave them just enough time to doze and then CRASH! The whole orchestra played a chord as loud as possible.

PLAYING

The game song "Kuma San" uses three pitches. Children in Japan sing "Kuma San" as they jump rope. The words tell you how to move.

TRACE the shape of the melody on the words Kuma San.

KUMA SAN
Honorable Bear

Japanese Folk Song
English Version by
Marilyn Davidson and
Kathy B. Sorensen

Japanese: く ま さん く ま さん ま わ れ み ぎ
Pronunciation: ku ma san ku ma san ma wa re mi gi
English: Ku - ma san, ku - ma san, turn your-self a - round.

く ま さん く ま さん りょう て を つい て
ku ma san ku ma san ryo te wo tsui te
Ku - ma san, ku - ma san, hands up - on the ground.

く ま さん く ま さん か た あ し あ げ て
ku ma san ku ma san ka ta a shi a ge te
Ku - ma san, ku - ma san, jump with one foot in the air.

く ま さん く ま さん さ よ う な ら
ku ma san ku ma san sa yo u na ra
Ku - ma san, ku - ma san, Sa - yo - u - na - ra.

WITH THREE PITCHES

SING "Kuma San" and touch your legs on the lowest pitch, your waist on the middle pitch, and your shoulders on the highest pitch.

Mi is the highest pitch.

Re is the middle pitch.

Do is the lowest pitch.

Pitches are written on a **staff** that has five lines and four spaces. The lines on a staff are numbered from the bottom up. What number is the top space? Top line?

Spaces

Lines

This staff shows the three pitches used in "Kuma San." In which space is *do*? *mi*? On which line is *re*?

do   re   mi

SING the tinted measures in "Rocky Mountain"
using *do re* and *mi*.

ROCKY
MOUNTAIN

Appalachian Folk Song

Verse

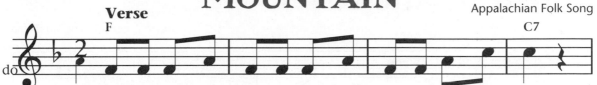

1. Rock - y moun-tain, rock - y moun-tain, rock - y moun-tain high,
2. Sun - ny val - ley, sun - ny val - ley, sun - ny val - ley low,
3. Storm-y o - cean, storm-y o - cean, storm-y o - cean wide,

When you're on that rock - y moun-tain, hang your head and cry.
When you're in that sun - ny val - ley, sing it soft and slow.
When you're on that deep blue sea, there's no place you can hide.

Refrain

Do, do, do, do, Do re - mem - ber me.

Do, do, do, do, Do re - mem - ber me.

You can see alike and different everywhere: on your clothes, in the playground, and even in this song.

ALIKE AND

Down by the River

African American Singing Game

1. Down by the riv - er two by two, ___
(2.) see you make a mo - tion two by two, ___
(3.) take an - oth - er part - ner two by two, ___

two by two, _ two by two. _ Down by the riv - er
two by two, _ two by two. _ Let me see you make a mo-tion
two by two, _ two by two. _ Now _ take an - oth - er part-ner

two by two, ___ now rise Sal - ly rise. 2. Let me
two by two, ___ now rise Sal - ly rise. 3.Now ___
two by two, ___ now rise Sal - ly rise.

Which measures in "Down by the River" are alike?

DIFFERENT

FINDING "DO" IN A DIFFERENT PLACE

Where is *do* in the song "Kuma San"?

Here is *do* in a different place–beneath
Line 1. *Re* and *mi* are always just above *do*.

SING "Down by the River" using
pitch syllable names.

The cook in this song is looking for what item?

DUMPLIN'S

West Indian Calypso Song
New Words and New Music Adaptation by
Massie Patterson and Sammy Heyward

Freely

"Cook-ie, _____ did you see a'-bod-y pass here?"

"No, my friend." "Cook-ie, _____ are you sure no-bod-y passed here?"

Refrain
Faster, with rhythm

"No, my friend." "Well {one/two} of my dump-lin's

gone." "Don't tell ___ me so!" {"One/"Two} of my dump-lin's

gone." "Don't tell __ me so!" {"One/"Two} of my dump-lin's gone!"

FIND the parts of "Dumplin's" that are alike.

Now find *do* in "Dumplin's."
Then sing the pattern *No, my friend* using pitch syllable names.

SIXTEEN HENS

The artist, Blanchard, is from the island of Haiti, part of the Caribbean Islands, where people first sang "Dumplin's." Blanchard used many shapes that are alike in this painting. Can you find three shapes that are alike? Three shapes that are different?

MUSICAL Choices

Haydn made many musical choices when he composed the "Surprise" Symphony. He chose:

rhythms

sounds and silences

pitches

higher and lower sounds

tone colors

the special sound of instruments and voices

You can make some choices about music, too! Start with the rhythm. Choose where the silence comes in the rhythm.

CLAP these rhythms. Then move to them. Move on the beats with sound. Rest on the beats with silence.

Which beat has no sound? What is the symbol for no sound on a beat?

CREATE your own rhythm patterns. Choose where to put the rest.

DYNAMICS: SOFT AND LOUD IN MUSIC

You can also make choices about **dynamics** in music. Dynamics are the softness or loudness of musical sounds.

LISTEN for soft and loud notes in the "Surprise" Symphony.

In music, *p* means *piano*. It means to sing or play the music *soft*. An *f* means *forte*. It means to sing or play the music *loud*.

What might *pp* mean?
What might *ff* mean?

SING this part of "Dumplin's" with these dynamics.

p
Well one of my dumplin's gone. Don't tell me so! *f*

p
One of my dumplin's gone. Don't tell me so! *f*

p
One of my dumplin's gone!

NOW sing "Dumplin's" with these dynamics.

f
Well one of my dumplin's gone. Don't tell me so! *p*

f
One of my dumplin's gone. Don't tell me so! *p*

f
One of my dumplin's gone!

THINK IT THROUGH

Sing "Dumplin's" with the dynamics you choose. Compare the ways you sang "Dumplin's." Which way do you like better? Why?

A MELODY FREEZE GAME

In this game you can move to the three pitches you know.

LISTEN to "Melody Freeze." Do you hear the last pitch of each phrase "freeze"? Freeze to show which pitch you hear.

A **_fermata_** () placed over a note
shows where the melody freezes. It tells
you to hold the note longer than usual.

**SING this melody with fermatas and
guess the song.**

The Hungry Waves

The hungry waves along the shore
Chase each other with a roar.

They raise their heads and, wide and high,
Toss their hair against the sky.

They show their teeth in rows of white
And open up their jaws to bite.

— Dorothy Aldis

THINK IT THROUGH

Which words of this poem might you
hold? Why did you choose these words?

GAME SONGS TO REMEMBER

You've learned some games that children in different countries play. What songs do these pictures remind you of?

Create a news program about the game songs. Choose someone to be the interviewer. Then form groups of three or four, and play one of the games. When the interviewer comes to your group, sing the song and show how the game is played.

CHECK IT OUT

1. You will hear a song with a drum playing along. What is the drum playing?

   a. the rhythm

   b. the beat

   c. changes from rhythm to beat

2. You will hear a song with a drum playing along. What is the drum playing?

   a. the rhythm

   b. the beat

   c. changes from rhythm to beat

3. How does this melody move?

   a. upward ↗

   b. downward ↘

   c. repeats on the same pitch →

   d. upward then downward ↗ ↘

4. Which rhythm do you hear?

5. What pitches do you hear?

   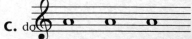

   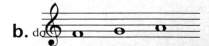

   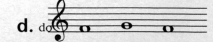

CREATE

Make Your Own Rhythm Pattern

Draw eight boxes on a piece of paper.

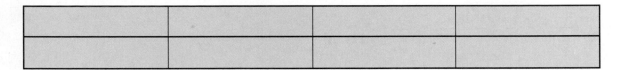

- Put 2 eighth notes (♪♪) in 2 or 3 boxes.
- Put a quarter note (♩) in 2 or 3 different boxes.
- Put a quarter rest (𝄽) in the other boxes.

CREATE a melody for your rhythm using the bells *do* (F), *re* (G), and *mi* (A).

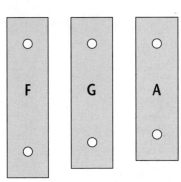

Add a surprise to your melody by playing a part of it loud.

Write

Think about the game songs that you like most. Write a letter to a child who lives in the country from which your favorite game comes.

- Describe what you enjoy about the game.
- Tell about a game that you play.

ENCORE
THE
ORCHESTRA

No one knows how music began. At first people might have created sounds by humming, clapping, or stamping. After a time, they might have started to make music by plucking or hitting some of their tools. Perhaps some of these tools became instruments, such as drums or flutes.

horn

LOOK at these pictures of early instruments.

How do you think each instrument was played? How do you think each one sounded?

drum

harp

flute

45

Montage of Orchestral Sounds

The orchestra has four families of instruments.

LISTEN for the sound of each family.

1. Woodwind family
2. String family
3. Percussion family
4. Brass family

Variations
on the Theme *Pop! Goes the Weasel*
by Lucien Caillet

 Lucien Caillet used an American folk song in his music for orchestra.

SING the song, then listen for the four instrument families in Caillet's music.

POP! GOES THE WEASEL

American Ring Game

All a-round the cob-bler's bench, The mon-key chased the wea-sel.

The mon-key said 'twas all __ in fun. Pop! goes the wea-sel.

BICYCLE RIDING

My feet rise
off the planet,
pedal wheels of steel
that sparkle as
they spin me through
the open space I feel
winging out
to galaxies
far beyond the sun,
where bicycles
are satellites
their orbits never done.

—*Sandra Liatsos*

GOIN

ON THE MOVE

You can take music with
you when you travel—in the car,
on a bus, bicycle riding, or even jogging.

LISTEN to "Jubilee," and tell how the
singer traveled.

Jubilee

Verse

Kentucky Play Party

1. All out on the old rail-road, All out on the sea;
2. Hard-est work I ev - er done, Work-ing on the farm.
3. If I had no horse at all, I'd be found a - crawl-in',
4. Some will come on Sat-ur-day night, Some will come on Sun-day;

All out on the old rail-road, Far as I could see.
Eas-i-est work I ev - er done was Swing-in' my true love's arm.
Up and down this rock - y road, Look - in' for my dar-lin'.
If you give 'em half a chance, They'll be back on Mon-day.

Refrain

Swing and turn, Ju - bi-lee, Live and learn, Ju - bi-lee.

SING "Jubilee." Pat with the beat on Lines 1 and 2.
Clap the rhythm of the words on Line 3.

50

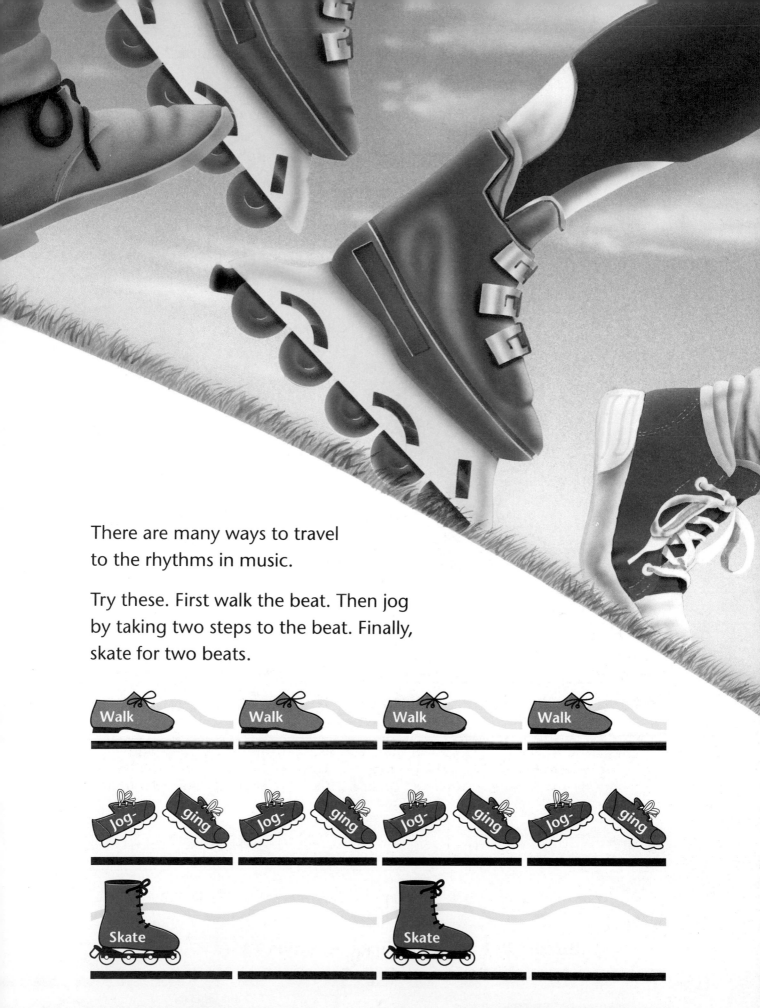

There are many ways to travel to the rhythms in music.

Try these. First walk the beat. Then jog by taking two steps to the beat. Finally, skate for two beats.

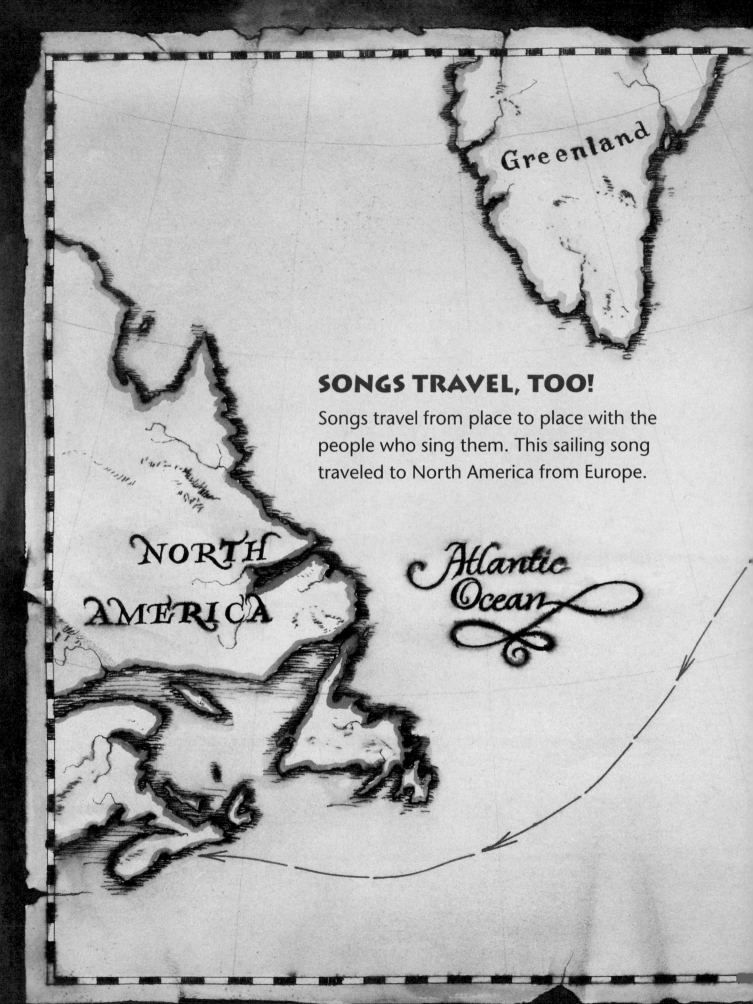

Greenland

SONGS TRAVEL, TOO!

Songs travel from place to place with the people who sing them. This sailing song traveled to North America from Europe.

NORTH AMERICA

Atlantic Ocean

LISTEN to "Turn the Glasses Over" and find places on the map that are included in the song.

Turn the Glasses Over

American Singing Game

I've been to Haarlem, I've been to Dover,
I've traveled this wide world all over,
Over, over, three times over,
Drink what you have to drink and turn the
    glasses over.
Sailing east, sailing west, Sailing o'er the ocean.
Better watch out when the boat begins to rock,
Or you'll lose your girl in the ocean.

LISTEN again, patting with the steady beat to find words that last for two beats.

DESIGNS IN MUSIC

Have you ever noticed train cars that are alike and different? Sometimes they make a design.

FIND the design made by the cars in this train. What kind of car would come next?

Many songs are designed using this pattern of same and different.

LISTEN to "Jubilee" to find its design. Point to the cars as you listen.

"Jubilee" is in **verse-refrain** form. Each **verse** has the same melody but different words. The **refrain** always has the same words and melody.

A VERSE-REFRAIN GAME

This game is about a vagabond, a person who travels from place to place. The game has the same verse-refrain form as "Jubilee."

LISTEN to the "Vagabond Game" as you pat the beat.

VAGABOND GAME

Verse:
My name is Amy, and I come from Alabama.
My name is Carlotta, and I come from California.
My name is Juan, and I come from Juarez.
My name is Miko, and I come from Mars.

Refrain:
As I went over the ocean,
As I went over the sea,
I came upon four vagabonds,
And this they said to me.

CREATE a verse to the "Vagabond Game" with three friends. Take turns saying a line of the verse, and then say the refrain together.

A VERSE-REFRAIN SONG

Here's a silly verse-refrain song. What verse
in the song makes you smile?

Autumn to May

Words and Music
by Paul Stookey
and Peter Yarrow

Verse

1. Oh, once I had a lit-tle dog, his col-or it was brown.
2. Oh, once I had a ti-ny frog, he wore a vest of red.
3. Oh, once I had a flock of sheep, they grazed up-on a fea-ther;
4. Oh, once I had a down-y swan, she was so ver-y frail,

I taught him how to whis-tle, ___ to sing and dance and run,
He leaned up-on a sil-ver cane, a top hat on his head.
I'd keep them in a mu-sic box from wind and rain-y wea-ther,
She sat up-on an oys-ter shell and hatched me out a snail,

His legs they were four-teen yards long, his ears so ver-y wide,
He'd speak of far-off plac-es, of things to see and do,
And ev'-ry day the sun would shine, they'd fly all through the town
The snail it changed in-to a bird, the bird to but-ter-fly,

A - round the world in half a day up - on him I could ride.
And all the kings and queens he'd met while sail-ing in a shoe.
To bring me back some gold - en rings and cand-y by the pound.
And he who tells a big - ger "tail" would have to tell a lie.

Refrain

Sing tar-ry o day, Sing _____ Au-tumn to May. _____

LISTEN to "Autumn to May" again,
singing on the refrain.

TRAVELING BY TRAIN

There are many ways to travel. Some ways are slower; some are faster. Sometimes you can tell how fast something is moving by listening.

THINK IT THROUGH

Describe how the sound of a train tells you it's moving slower or faster.

In music, the speed of the beat can be slow or fast. The speed of the beat is called **tempo.**

Meet STEVE REICH

Steve Reich (b. 1936) was born in New York. He composed the piece "Different Trains" to sound and feel like a train traveling. First he recorded the voices of his governess and a Pullman porter. He then mixed these voices with string instruments and whistle sounds to create a piece that sounds like a train moving.

LISTENING

Different Trains *by Steve Reich*

LISTENING MAP *Follow this listening map as you listen to "Different Trains."*

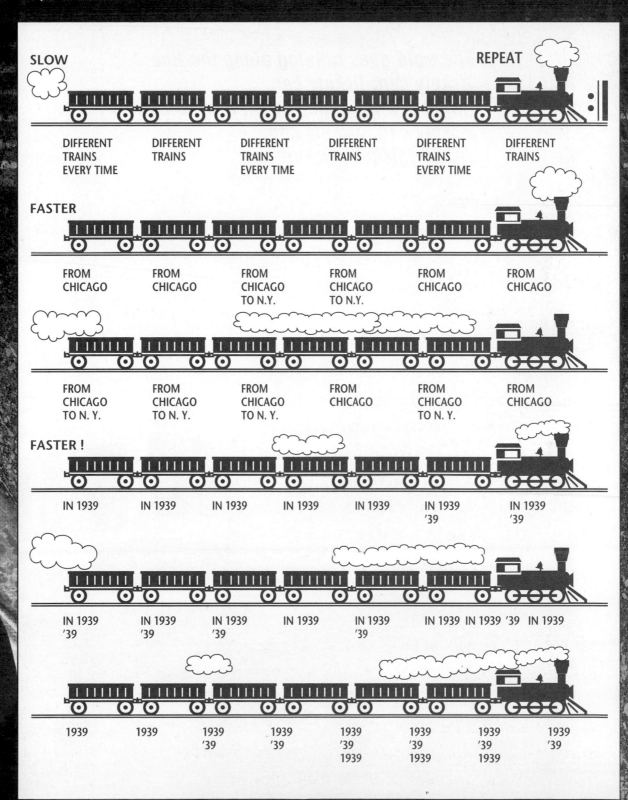

SLOW

DIFFERENT TRAINS EVERY TIME DIFFERENT TRAINS DIFFERENT TRAINS EVERY TIME DIFFERENT TRAINS DIFFERENT TRAINS EVERY TIME DIFFERENT TRAINS

REPEAT

FASTER

FROM CHICAGO FROM CHICAGO FROM CHICAGO TO N.Y. FROM CHICAGO TO N.Y. FROM CHICAGO FROM CHICAGO

FROM CHICAGO TO N. Y. FROM CHICAGO TO N. Y. FROM CHICAGO TO N. Y. FROM CHICAGO FROM CHICAGO TO N. Y. FROM CHICAGO

FASTER !

IN 1939 IN 1939 IN 1939 IN 1939 IN 1939 IN 1939 '39 IN 1939 '39

IN 1939 '39 IN 1939 '39 IN 1939 '39 IN 1939 IN 1939 '39 IN 1939 IN 1939 '39 IN 1939

1939 1939 1939 '39 1939 '39 1939 '39 1939 1939 '39 1939 1939 '39 1939 1939 '39 1939

LISTEN to this speech piece to find what words sound like a passing train.

Jickety Can

Anonymous

The train goes running along the line.
Jickety can, jickety can,
I wish it were mine, I wish it were mine!
Jickety can, Jickety can.
Jickety, jickety, jickety can.

Say "Jickety Can" as if the train is leaving the station. How does the tempo change?

Musicians use the word **accelerando** to describe the tempo speeding up.

CREATE your own train music. Ask a partner to say "Jickety Can" as you speak your own train sounds in an eight-beat rhythm pattern.

MANCHESTER VALLEY

Joseph Pickett's painting of a train shows movement. Can you hear the *jickety can, jickety can* or *toot, toot* in this scene? What tempo and mood does the painting suggest?

TRAVELING RHYTHMS

Take a journey aboard a train in this folk song from Venezuela. You'll be traveling over bridges and through tunnels on your way to the capital.

LISTEN to "El tren" and brush your hands to the beat.

El tren
THE TRAIN

Venezuelan Folk Song

Spanish: "Pá Ca - ra - cas" di - ce el tren cuan - do
Pronunciation: pa ka ɾa kas ði sel tɾen kwan ðo
English: "To Ca - ra - cas," says the train when it's

vie - ne de Los Te - ques. "Pá Ca - ra - cas" di - ce el
βye ne ðe los te kes pa ka ɾa kas ði sel
com - ing from Los Te - ques. "To Ca - ra - cas," says the

tren cuan - do vie - ne de Los Te - ques. Pá Ca -
tɾen kwan ðo βye ne ðe los te kes pa ka
train when it's com - ing from Los Te - ques. To Ca -

ra - cas, pá Ca - ra - cas, siem - pre lle - ni - to de
ɾa kas pa ka ɾa kas syem pɾe ye ni to ðe
ra - cas, to Ca - ra - cas, al - ways ver - y full of

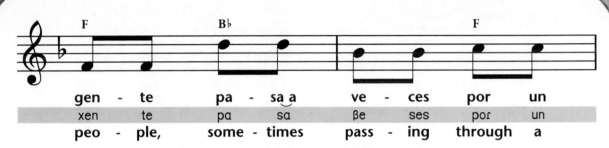

gen - te   pa - sa_a   ve - ces   por   un
xen   te   pa   sa   ße   ses   poɾ   un
peo - ple,   some - times   pass - ing   through a

tu - nel   y_o - tras   ve - ces   por   un   puen - te.
tu   nel   yo   tɾas   ße   ses   poɾ   un   pwen   te
tun - nel, some - times   pass - ing o - ver   bridg - es.

2. **When it's going through a tunnel,**
   it goes very, very slowly.
   (Repeat)

   Very gently, very slowly,
   so the people won't be frightened.
   (Repeat)

3. **When it crosses over bridges,**
   it begins to go much faster.
   (Repeat)

   Hurry, hurry, hurry, hurry,
   we're arriving in Caracas!
   (Repeat)

After your train ride, try reading a new traveling rhythm. The **tie** (͜) tells you to hold the sound for two beats.

1.
walk,   walk,   skate, _____   walk,   walk,   skate _____

2.
walk,   walk,   walk,   walk,   skate, _____   skate _____

You can also write ♩ ͜ ♩ with a **half note** (♪)

PAT with the beat as you say these rhythms.

1.

walk,   walk,   skate,   walk,   walk,   skate

2.

walk,   walk,   walk,   walk,   skate,   skate

Find the line in "Turn the Glasses Over" that has both Rhythm 1 and Rhythm 2.

American Singing Game

Verse

I've been to Haar-lem, I've been to Do-ver,

I've trav-eled this wide world all o-ver,

O-ver, o-ver, three times o-ver,

Drink what you have to drink and turn the glass-es o-ver.

Refrain

Sail-ing east, sail-ing west, Sail-ing o'er the o-cean,

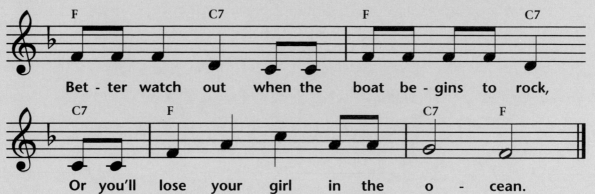

Bet - ter watch out when the boat be - gins to rock,

Or you'll lose your girl in the o - cean.

Find a partner and perform this movement called "wringing the dishrag."

Travel around the room with your partner as you listen to "Turn the Glasses Over." When you hear the words *turn the glasses over,* "wring the dishrag."

Take the Melody Up,

Up, and Away!

Have you ever traveled in a hot-air balloon? Take a melody up, up, and away by reading pitches higher than *do re mi*.

do re mi

Look at the beginning of "Jubilee."

All out on the old rail-road, All out on the sea;

SING *old railroad.* **What pitch syllables are these notes?**

Are the other notes higher or lower than *do re mi*?

TWO PITCHES HIGHER THAN "MI"

The two pitches higher than *do re mi* in "Jubilee" are **so** and **la**.

do   re   mi   so   la

What space is *so* in? What line is *la* on?

SING the first line of "Jubilee" and show the pitches with these movements.

la touch your head

so touch your shoulders

mi touch your waist

re touch your thighs

do touch your knees

68

SING "Deta, Deta" in Japanese.

Deta, Deta
THE MOON

Japanese
Children's Song
Collected and Transcribed by
Kathy B. Sorensen

Japanese:	で	た	で	た	つ	き	が
Pronunciation:	de	ta	de	ta	tsu	ki	ga
English:	**Now**	**the**	**moon**	**is**	**com -**	**ing**	**out!**

	ま	—	る	い	ま	—	る
	ma		ɾu	i	ma		ɾu
	Big	**and**	**round,**	**so**	**big**	**and**	**round,**

い	ま	ん	ま	る	い
i	ma	ŋ	ma	ɾu	i
as	**round ___**		**as**	**a**	**tray.**

ぼ	—	ん	の	よ	う	な	つ	き	が
bo		ŋ	no	yo		na	tsu	ki	ga
Big ___		**and ___**		**round**		**just**	**like**	**a**	**tray.**

2. Now the moon is hiding!
   Gone away, O gone away,
   Behind the clouds.
   Black as ink, behind the clouds.

Find *do* in "Deta, Deta." Then find *re mi so* and *la.*

SING "Deta, Deta" using pitch syllables and movements.

TONE COLORS

Imagine you travel to the moon. Do you suppose the sounds would be the same as on Earth? Imagine how the tone colors of your voice and instruments might change.

LISTENING

Silver Moon *by Kitaro*

An electronic instrument called a **synthesizer** *can create and play many tone colors. Kitaro uses the synthesizer to write music. He imagined sounds of the moon and wrote a piece called "Silver Moon."*

LISTEN to "Silver Moon" and describe the tone colors. Move differently for each tone color.

How would you describe the mood or feeling of "Silver Moon"?

OF THE MOON

TONE COLOR WITH WORDS

If you wanted to write a poem about "Silver Moon," you might write a haiku.

A **haiku** is a special kind of poem created in Japan long ago. A haiku usually has 17 syllables! Many haiku are about nature.

READ this haiku and imagine the scene it describes.

Clink, an iced branch falls.

I see the shattered moonlight

Scatter at my feet.

—KAZUE MIZUMURA

CREATE sounds with your voice to go with the haiku.

PERFORM your vocal tone colors as a friend reads the haiku.

What rhythm instruments could you use to play with this haiku?

MOONLIGHT ON THE RIVER AT SEBA

The artist Hiroshige blends colors and images to give his colored wood-block print a quiet, peaceful tone. What instruments would you choose to reflect the feeling of the art? Why?

SOUNDS OF TRAVELING

You can use your voice to make louder and softer sounds. Musicians know how loud or soft to play the music by signs called **dynamics.** Dynamics are written above or below the music.

p	soft
pp	softer
ppp	softest
f	loud
ff	louder
fff	loudest

Crescendo means to play or sing louder, little by little.

Decrescendo means to play or sing softer, little by little.

SAY "Jickety Can" following the dynamics above the lines.

f
The train goes running along the line.

p
Jickety can, jickety can

f
I wish it were mine. I wish it were mine!

p
Jickety can, jickety can

ppp ——————— *fff*
Jickety, jickety, jickety can.

THINK IT THROUGH
Write the words to "Jickety Can" on a piece of paper and add your own dynamics. Say "Jickety Can" with your dynamics.

COMPARE the performances. Which do you like best? Why?

SPEAKING A CANON

These two trains are traveling at the same speed, but one started before the other.

SAY "Jickety Can" in two groups. One group starts before the other.

In music, this is called a **canon**.

LISTENING

Night Watch
by Anthony Holborne

LISTEN to "Night Watch," and move to show the dynamic changes you hear.

Do you take pictures or buy postcards when you travel? Pictures and postcards can help you to remember your trip.

Pictures can help you to remember songs, too. Try using the pictures on this page to remember all of the words to "Autumn to May."

NEW YORK, NY 100
PM
19 JAN

LISTEN to "Autumn to May" and figure out the correct verse-refrain order for the pictures. Remember, the refrain will repeat four times, once after every verse.

SING TARRY O DAY SING AUTUMN TO MAY

SING "Autumn to May" and point to the pictures in the correct order.

CLAP the rhythm below. Which sound takes up two beat boxes?

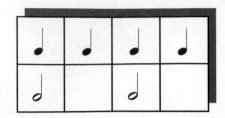

In this rhythm, the half notes and quarter notes traveled to a new place.

CLAP this new rhythm.

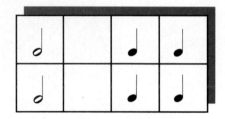

CREATE your own eight-beat rhythm pattern.

Draw eight boxes, like the ones below, on a piece of paper. Then, choose either a quarter note or a half note to fill the boxes. Remember, a half note takes two boxes.

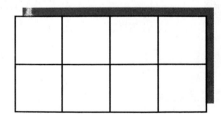

PERFORM your rhythms on unpitched instruments.

SOLVE THE MYSTERY!

This song is missing its melody. Use the rhythms below to tell what song it's from.

Which is the mystery song?

- "Autumn to May"
- "Jubilee"
- "Turn the Glasses Over"
- "Deta, Deta"

REVIEW

A RETURN TRIP

Take a musical journey by reviewing the songs you know. Begin by saying the refrain of the "Vagabond Game."

Refrain:
As I went over the ocean,
As I went over the sea,
I came upon four vagabonds,
And this they said to me.

Board a train in Venezuela as you sing "El tren."

Say the "Vagabond Game" refrain again, then sail on a clipper ship as you sing "Turn the Glasses Over."

Say the refrain again and then sing verse 2 of "Jubilee."

"Jubilee" is a verse-refrain song. What words start the refrain?

Finally, take a rest under the moon as you sing "Deta, Deta."

#

CHECK IT OUT

1. In which order do you hear the verse and refrain?

   a. refrain - verse - verse - refrain   **c.** verse - verse - refrain - refrain

   b. verse - refrain - verse - refrain   **d.** refrain - verse - refrain - verse

2. Which rhythm do you hear?

   a.    **c.**

   b. 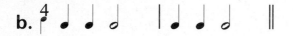   **d.**

3. What pitches do you hear?

   a.    **c.**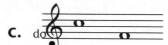

   b.    **d.**

4. Which melody do you hear?

   a.    **c.**

   b. 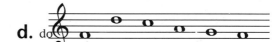   **d.**

84

CREATE

Make Your Own Traveling Melody

CLAP this rhythm. Say "walk" for ♩ "jogging" for ♫ and "skate" for ♩ Say nothing on 𝄽

CREATE a melody for the rhythm using the pitches *do re mi so* and *la*.

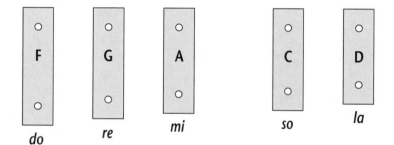

F	G	A	C	D
do	re	mi	so	la

Choose a partner and take turns playing each other's melody.

PERFORM your melodies in verse-refrain order. **One person plays his or her melody. Then the class sings the refrain of "Jubilee." Repeat until everyone's melody is played.**

Write

Decide on a place you would like to visit. Write a postcard to a friend. Describe the place and how you got there.

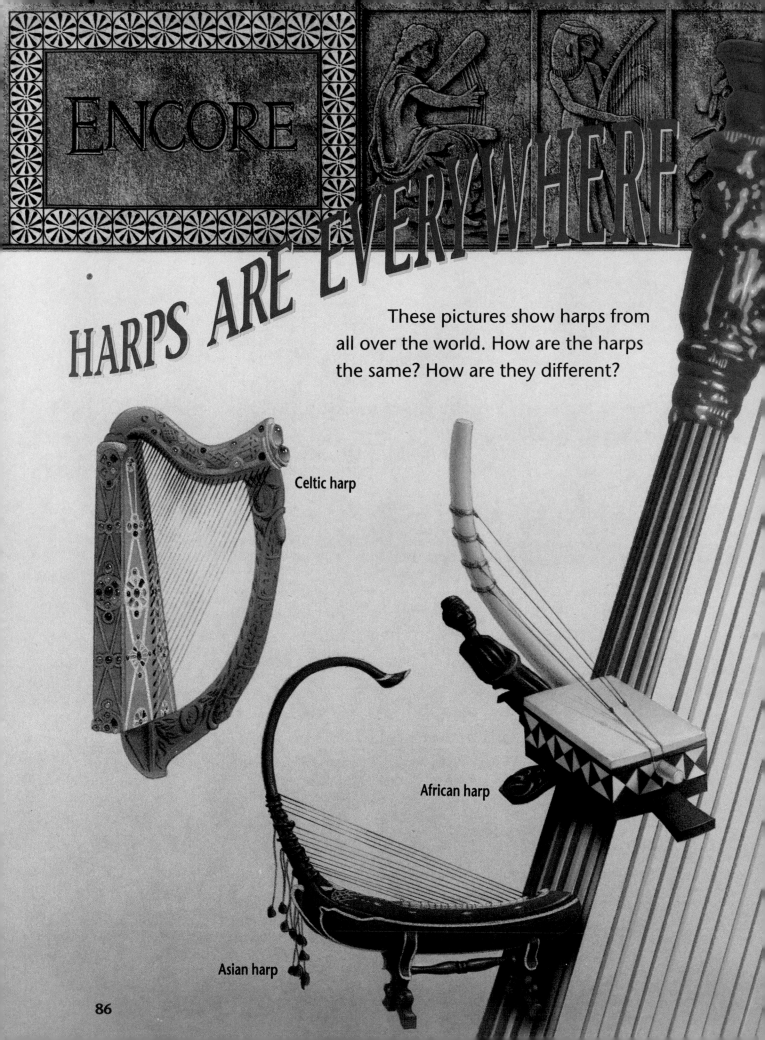

ENCORE

HARPS ARE EVERYWHERE

These pictures show harps from all over the world. How are the harps the same? How are they different?

Celtic harp

African harp

Asian harp

The harp is one of the oldest instruments in the world and the oldest instrument in the string family. *Archeologists,* people who study ancient ways of life, have found pieces of harps in Egyptian tombs that are 5,000 years old!

European orchestral harp

MEET ALFREDO ROLANDO ORTIZ

Alfredo Rolando Ortiz borrowed a harp and took his first lesson from a friend. They were both 13 years old. Each week Ortiz carried his harp over many hills for his lesson. His parents did not think his interest would last, but he surprised them!

LISTEN to Alfredo Rolando Ortiz as he talks about his career as a harpist and plays *"El pajaro campana"* (The Bell Bird).

The harp can make many different sounds. The soft
sounds of the harp have often reminded people of angels.

LISTEN to the sounds of the harp in this song.

Oh Lord, I Want
Two Wings

African American Spiritual

1. Oh, Lord, I want two wings to cov - er my face, ___
2. Oh, Lord, I want two gold - en shoes for my feet, ___
3. Oh, Lord, I want a gold - en harp ___ to play, ___

Oh, Lord, I want two wings to cov - er my face, ___
Oh, Lord, I want two gold - en shoes for my feet, ___
Oh, Lord, I want a gold - en harp ___ to play, ___

Oh, Lord, I want two wings to cov - er my face, ___
Oh, Lord, I want two gold - en shoes for my feet, ___
Oh, Lord, I want a gold - en harp ___ to play, ___

And the world can do me no harm. ___

EVERYDAY MUSIC

THE WORLD IS
DAY-BREAKING

What are days for?

Days are where we live.

They come, they wake us

Time and time over.

They are to be happy in:

Where can we live but days?

—*Sekiya Miyoshi*

EVERYDAY FOLK MUSIC

Many of the songs you sing every day were first sung hundreds of years ago. If we don't know who created them, they're called **folk songs.** Some folk songs tell stories. The folk song "Charlie" comes from the British Isles. It tells about "Bonnie Prince Charlie," who tried to claim the British throne in 1745.

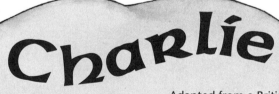

Charlie

Adapted from a British Folk Song

1. Step her to your weev'ly wheat, and step her to your barley,
   Step her to you weev'ly wheat to bake a cake for Charlie.

   Refrain
   Over the river to feed my sheep, Over the river, Charlie!
   Over the river to feed my sheep, And measure up my barley!

2. Over and over, ten times over, Charlie is a rover;
   Take your partner by the hands and wring the dishrag over.

   Refrain

Here's another piece that tells about an everyday event–making a favorite food! You might hear this game on playgrounds in Texas, Mexico, and Ecuador. It tells about a chocolate sauce called *mole*. The sauce is served with rice, tomatoes, chicken, and chili peppers.

CLAP the rhythm of the words to find a line that has the same rhythm as *Bate, bate, chocolate.*

BATE, BATE

Mexican Game

Bate, bate, chocolate,
Con arroz y con tomate.
Uno, dos, tres, CHO-,
Uno, dos, tres, CO-,
Uno, dos, tres, LA-,
Uno, dos, tres, TE,
Chocolate,
Chocolate,
Chocolate,
Chocolate.

EQUAL AND UNEQUAL RHYTHMS

"Charlie" and "Bate, bate" are both performed to a steady beat, but the rhythm of the words sounds and feels different. Find out why.

CLAP the rhythm of the words in "Bate, bate."

Ba- te, ba- te, cho- co- la- te,

CLAP the rhythm of the words in "Charlie."

Step her to your weev'- ly wheat and

COMPARE the rhythms of the words. Which rhythm has two unequal (long-short) sounds to each beat? Two equal (short-short) sounds to each beat?

The folk song "Veinte y tres" comes from sheepherders in New Mexico.

LISTEN to "Veinte y tres" and pat the rhythm of the words.

U-   na͜y U-   na͜y U-   na͜y U   na͜y

Is the rhythm of "Veinte y tres" equal or unequal?

SONG SHAPES

Some folk songs are created
from the words of everyday games.

LISTEN to "Rocky Road" and find
the words *red light, green light.* Can
you find another game in this song?

Rocky Road

Based on Lyrics Adapted and Arranged by
Peter Yarrow, Paul Stookey, and Albert Grossman

Verse 1: Red light, green light, 'round the town,
Found a penny on the ground,
Met a friend I never knowed,
Walkin' down old Rocky Road.

Refrain: Red, green, old Rocky Road,
Tell me what you see,
Red, green, old Rocky Road,
Tell me what you see,
Tell me inside out, Tell me upside down,
All around the block, all around the town.

Verse 2: Hey, Jimmy Higgins your name's been called,
Come and stand behind the wall.
Red light, green light, come and play,
Little Miss Jenny, you're it today.   *Refrain*

Ending: One p'tato, two p'tato, three p'tato, four,
Cross the line, close the door.

96

Tracing the shape of the melody can help you to learn a new song.

TRACE the shape of this part of "Rocky Road" when you hear it.

For hundreds of years people had to get water from wells by drawing it up in a bucket. The folk song "Draw a Bucket of Water" tells of this everyday chore. It comes from the Georgia Sea Islands.

SING the first part of the song as you pretend to pull a bucket of water from the well. Sing the ending as if you are surprised!

Draw a Bucket of Water

African American
Singing Game

Refrain: Draw a bucket of water
For my only daughter.

1. There's none in the bunch, we're all out the bunch,
   You go under, sister Sally. *Refrain*
2. There's one in the bunch, and three out the bunch,
   You go under, sister Sally. *Refrain*
3. There's two in the bunch, and two out the bunch,
   You go under, sister Sally. *Refrain*
4. There's three in the bunch, and one out the bunch,
   You go under, sister Sally.

Ending: Frog in the bucket and I can't get him out.
Repeat 8 times

TRACE the shape of the melody of "Draw a Bucket of Water," and match the shape to one of the patterns below.

1. Draw a buck-et of wa-ter

2. Draw a buck-et of wa-ter

3. Draw a buck-et of wa-ter

Conducting Too!

Sometimes folk songs like "Draw a Bucket of Water" are performed while working. The movements become part of the song.

PERFORM the movements for "Draw a Bucket of Water" as you sing the song.

You'll pretend to pull water out of the well, make a bucket with your friends, and act surprised at what's in the bucket besides water!

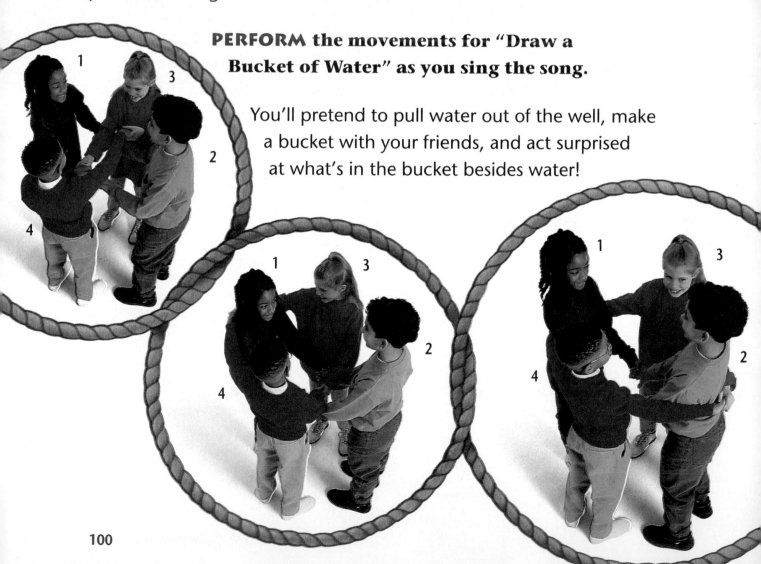

You can be the conductor! First practice by patting with the beat as you listen to this speech piece.

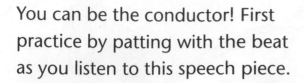 # Rattlesnake Skipping Song

Mississauga rattlesnakes **Eat** brown bread.
Mississauga rattlesnakes **Fall** down dead.
If you catch a caterpillar, **Feed** him apple juice; But
If you catch a rattlesnake, **Turn** him loose!

—Dennis Lee

CONDUCT in sets of two as you listen again. Think *one* on the strong beat, the downbeat, and *two* on the weak beat, the upbeat.

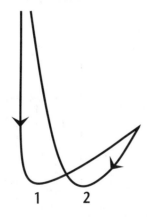

Spotlight on
Arcangelo Corelli

The Granger Collection

Arcangelo Corelli (1653–1713) lived in Italy about three hundred years ago. He loved to play the violin, and he wrote music for many different instruments. The king and queen invited Corelli to live in the royal palace, where he wrote and played music just for them.

 LISTENING

Gigue (excerpt) from Sonata for Violin and Continuo
by Arcangelo Corelli

 LISTENING MAP   Now it's time to conduct the orchestra. Show the beats or tap on the pictures below as you listen to this music.

1 2	1 2	1 2	1 2	1 2	1 2	1 2	1 2

1 2	1 2	1 2	1 2	1 2	1 2	1 2	1 2

1 2	1 2	1 2	1 2	1 2	1 2	1 2

Pat Me a Song

In an unequal rhythm, one sound is long and one sound is short. In the rhythm below, the first sound is longer than the second.

♩ ♪♩ ♪

FIND this quarter-eighth pattern in "Veinte y tres."

VEINTE Y TRES

TWENTY THREE

New Mexican Game Song

Spanish: U - na y u - na y   u - na y u - na y   u - na y dos son   tres.
Pronunciation: u na yu na   yu na yu na   yu nai ðos on   tres
English: **One and one, and   one and one, and   one and two are   three;**

Con - ta - ban y con - ta - ban y con - ta - ban al   re - vés.
kon ta βan i kon ta βan i kon ta βan al r̄e βes
They count-ed and they   count-ed, and they   count-ed in   re - verse.

Con - ta - ban y con - ta - ban y con - ta - ban vein - te y tres.
kon ta βan i kon ta βan i kon ta βan βein te tres
They count-ed and they   count-ed, and they   count-ed twen-ty - three.

CHARLIE'S BACK!

You can find the quarter-eighth pattern many times in this song.

CLAP the rhythm of "Charlie."

Step her to   your weev'-ly wheat, and   step her to   your bar - ley,

Step her to   your weev'-ly wheat to   bake   a cake for   Char - lie.

Find the places where the quarter-eighth pattern stops.

The note above these words is a **dotted quarter note** (♩.) In "Charlie," the dotted quarter note gets the beat. The meter sign ($^2_{♩.}$) at the beginning of the song tells you that there are two beats in each measure.

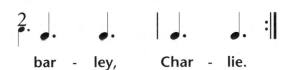

bar - ley,   Char - lie.

A beat with no sound in $\frac{2}{.}$ meter is called a **dotted quarter rest** $(\xi\cdot)$

CLAP this pattern.

Take turns playing the pattern on a tambourine as your class sings "Charlie."

CHARLIE

Adapted from a British Folk Song

Verse

1. Step her to your weev'-ly wheat, and step her to your bar - ley,
2. O-ver and o - ver, ten times o - ver, Char-lie is a ro - ver;

Step her to your weev'-ly wheat to bake a cake for Char - lie.
Take your part-ner by the hands and wring the dish-rag o - ver.

Refrain

O-ver the riv-er to feed my sheep, O-ver the riv - er, Char - lie!

O-ver the riv-er to feed my sheep, And mea-sure up my bar - ley!

CLAP these rhythms in $\frac{2}{4}$ meter.

1. $\frac{2}{4}$ ♩ ♩ ♪♪ ♪♩ | ♩. 𝄽 ‖

2. $\frac{2}{4}$ ♩. ♩. | ♩ ♪♩. ‖

LISTEN for these rhythms in this song.

Row, Row, Row Your Boat

Traditional Round

Row, row, row your boat
Gently down the stream;
Merrily, merrily, merrily, merrily,
Life is but a dream.

Which rhythm matches *Row, row, row your boat?*
Gently down the stream?
Life is but a dream?

THINK IT THROUGH

Use the two rhythms above to create a speech piece. Choose words to say with the rhythms. Perform your pieces with classroom instruments.

TWO NEW PITCHES IN THE WELL

In this song, you'll find two new pitches.

FIND the pitches *do re* and *mi* as you listen and trace the first line of "Draw a Bucket of Water."

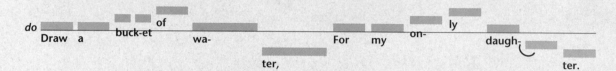

do Draw a buck-et of wa- ter, For my on- ly daugh- ter.

The two new pitches you found are called low **la** and low **so**. In this song, low *so* is on a **ledger line**, a line added below the staff.

do so, la, do re mi

You also found a curved line called a slur. A **slur** ($\smile$) tells you to sing a syllable on more than one pitch.

Find a slur over the word *daughter*.

DRAW A BUCKET OF WATER

African American Play-Party Song

1.–4. Draw a buck-et of wa - ter For my on - ly daugh - ter.

There's { none in the bunch, we're all out the bunch,
one in the bunch, and three out the bunch,
two in the bunch, and two out the bunch,
three in the bunch, and one out the bunch,

(Four times)

You ___ go un - der, sis - ter Sal - ly.

Faster

Frog in the buck - et and I can't get him out,

Frog in the buck - et and I can't get him out,

Frog in the buck - et and I can't get him out,

Frog in the buck - et and I can't get him out.

Written and adapted by Bessie Jones. Collected and Edited by Alan Lomax. TRO · © Copyright 1972 Ludlow Music, Inc., New York, NY. Used by permission.

"Draw a Bucket of Water" and "Now Let Me Fly" were first sung by enslaved Africans brought to America to work. "Now Let Me Fly" is a religious folk song called a **spiritual.** Imagine being forced to work all day in a large field under a hot sun. Why might you sing "Now Let Me Fly"?

Now Let Me Fly

Refrain

African American Spiritual

Now let me fly, _____ Now let me fly, _____

Now let me fly ___ way up high, _ Way in the mid-dle of the air.

Verse

Way down yon - der in the mid - dle of the field,

See me work - ing at the char - i-ot wheel.

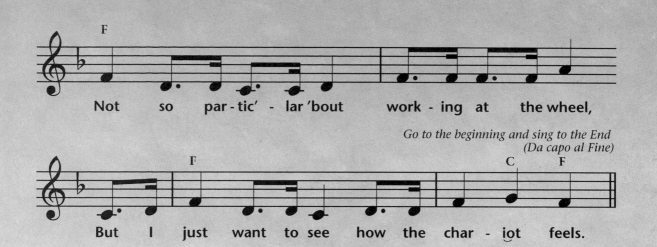

Not so par-tic'-lar 'bout work-ing at the wheel,

Go to the beginning and sing to the End
(Da capo al Fine)

But I just want to see how the char-iot feels.

CREATE your own melody for the verse of "Now Let Me Fly." Use these pitches.

la
so
mi
re
do
la₁
so₁

For many years most folk songs were not written down. Instead, they were passed from singer to singer. People often changed the songs a little each time they sang them. For this reason, many folk songs have come down to us in different versions. Here are two versions of the song "Charlie."

SING "Charlie" with an unequal rhythm in ²⅃· meter.

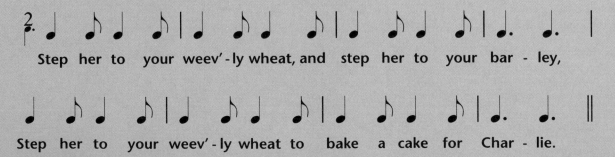

"ARLIES"

Now try "Charlie" a different way!

SING "Charlie" with an equal rhythm in $\frac{2}{4}$ meter.

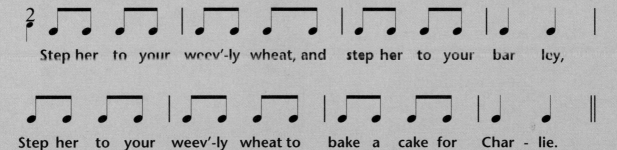

Step her to your weev'-ly wheat, and step her to your bar ley,

Step her to your weev'-ly wheat to bake a cake for Char - lie.

THINK IT THROUGH

How does the $\frac{2}{4}$ meter make the song feel different?
How would you move differently when the song is
in $\frac{2}{4}$ meter?

Sentry Box
and
Andrew and His Cutty Gun

Traditional Fife and Drum Music

Fife and drum music has a lively rhythm. This music was often played to help soldiers march together. Today, you can hear it in parades.

PAT each rhythm as you listen to these two pieces.

COMPARE the two pieces.

Which one feels like it is in equal meter? In unequal meter?

MOVE to show the meters.

Skip to the unequal meter.
Step-hop to the equal meter.

You can step-hop or skip to "Bate, bate," too!

**MOVE to "Bate, bate" in equal ($^2_{\text{♪}}$) meter,
then in unequal ($^2_{\text{♪.}}$) meter.**

BATE, BATE

Mexican Game

**Bate, bate, chocolate,
Con arroz y con tomate,
Uno, dos, tres, CHO-,
Uno, dos, tres, CO-,
Uno, dos, tres, LA-,
Uno, dos, tres, TE,
Chocolate, Chocolate,
Chocolate, Chocolate.**

Match these rhythms in $^2_{\text{♪.}}$ to a line of
"Bate, bate."

ROAD SIGNS

In this song the phrase *Red, green, old Rocky Road, Tell me what you see* repeats. A **repeat sign** (𝄆 𝄇) tells you to repeat this phrase of the song.

FIND the repeat signs in "Rocky Road," and then sing the song.

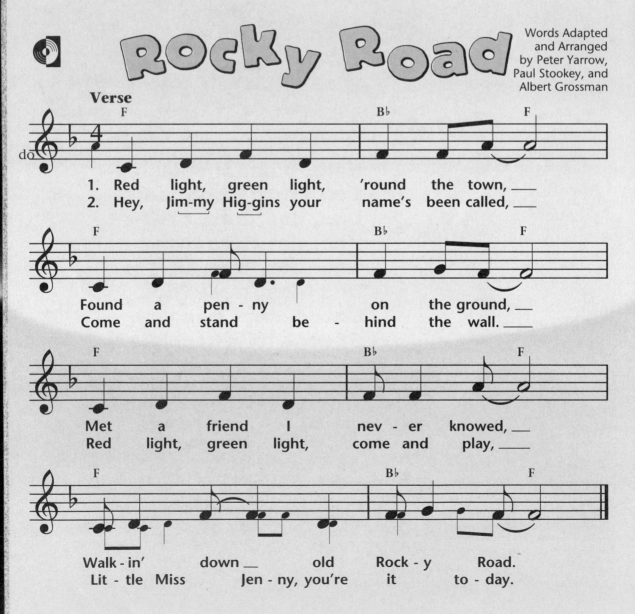

Rocky Road

Words Adapted and Arranged by Peter Yarrow, Paul Stookey, and Albert Grossman

Verse

1. Red light, green light, 'round the town, ___
2. Hey, Jim-my Hig-gins your name's been called, ___

Found a pen - ny on the ground, ___
Come and stand be - hind the wall. ___

Met a friend I nev - er knowed, ___
Red light, green light, come and play, ___

Walk - in' down ___ old Rock - y Road.
Lit - tle Miss Jen - ny, you're it to - day.

Refrain

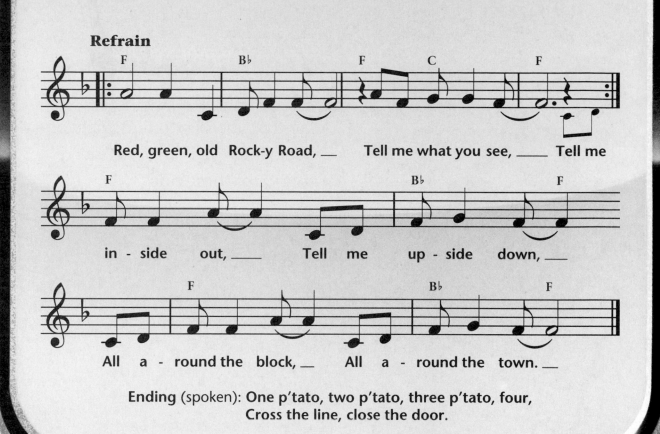

Red, green, old Rock-y Road, __ Tell me what you see, ___ Tell me in - side out, ___ Tell me up - side down, __ All a - round the block, __ All a - round the town. __

Ending (spoken): **One p'tato, two p'tato, three p'tato, four,**
Cross the line, close the door.

In music, a pattern that repeats over and over is called an **ostinato**.

PERFORM this rhythm ostinato by snapping the rhythm of the words.

Rock - y Road.

PLAY this rhythm ostinato on an instrument as you sing "Rocky Road."

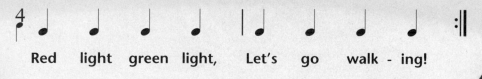

Red light green light, Let's go walk - ing!

REPEATED SOUNDS

Are there rides at the park or the fair that you like to ride again and again? Can you imagine the sounds of these rides?

LISTENING

Three Rides at the Park *by Linda Williams*

LISTEN to "Three Rides at the Park." Match each one of the ostinatos you hear to one of the three rides pictured.

CREATE a movement for each ostinato with a friend. Perform your movements as you listen again.

You can sing an ostinato, too! A short melody that repeats over and over is called a **melodic ostinato.**

SING this melodic ostinato and follow the repeat sign.

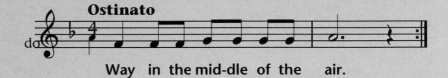

Ostinato

Way in the mid-dle of the air.

Take turns singing the ostinato as your class sings "Now Let Me Fly."

SING!
High, Low, and In Between

SING the refrain of "Now Let Me Fly."

Sing way down low,

Now let me fly, _____

way up high,

Now let me fly, _____

and way in the middle of the air.

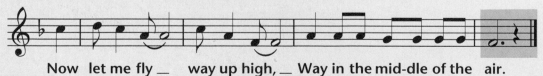

Now let me fly _ way up high, _ Way in the mid-dle of the air.

SING the refrain again using pitch syllables.

Name the pitches in the tinted measures.

SING the refrain of
"Now Let Me Fly" again.

Hold your hands on the floor
when you sing low *so.*

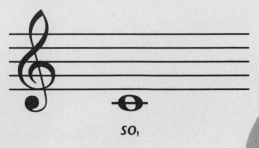

*so*₁

Hold your hands above your
head when you sing *so.*

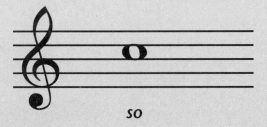

so

Hold your hands on your
waist when you sing *do.*

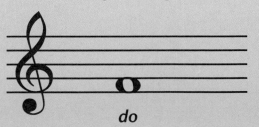

do

Play a game of "Musical
Red Light" and freeze to
show which pitch you hear.

MISSING PITCHES

Charlie lost some notes from his song. Help Charlie find the missing notes.

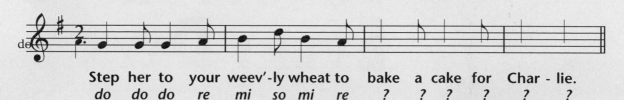

Step her to your weev'-ly wheat to bake a cake for Char - lie.
do   do do   re   mi   so   mi   re   ?   ?   ?   ?   ?   ?

Use these pitch stairs to help you name the missing pitches.

la

so

mi

re

do

la₁

so₁

SONGS FOR EVERY DAY

Match these song titles to the pictures.
"Charlie"
"Bate, bate"
"Rocky Road"
"Draw a Bucket of Water"
"Veinte y tres"

Make up a silly story that
includes all of these song titles.
Start your story this way:

**One day I went to "Draw a Bucket
of Water" from the well when . . .**
or
**I was making popcorn
when my friend
"Charlie" said . . .**

Read the story
and sing the songs
when you come to their titles.

124

CHECK IT OUT

1. Which of these has an equal rhythm?

   a.   **b.**   **c.**

2. Which of these has an unequal rhythm?

   a.   **b.**   **c.**

3. Which rhythm do you hear?

   a.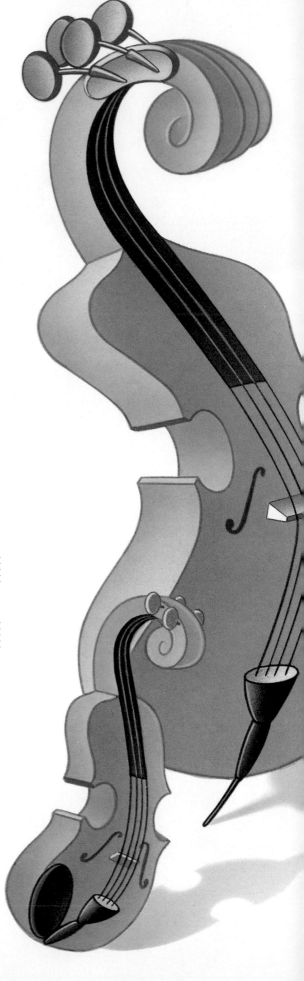

   b.

   c.

   d.

4. Choose the pitches you hear.

   a.   **c.**

   b.   **d.**

5. Which melody do you hear?

   a.

   b.

   c.

   d.

CREATE

Make Your Own Everyday Music

Combine some movements to make your own eight-beat pattern. Draw these lines on a piece of paper.

Rhythm

Movement

Put one of these on each line.

Rhythm
Movement

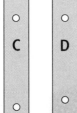	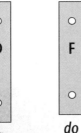	
walk	skip - ping	rest

Use the bells *so, la, do re mi so la* to add a melody. Begin and end on *do* (F).

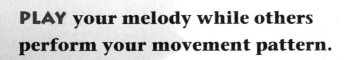

so, la, do re mi so la

PLAY your melody while others perform your movement pattern.

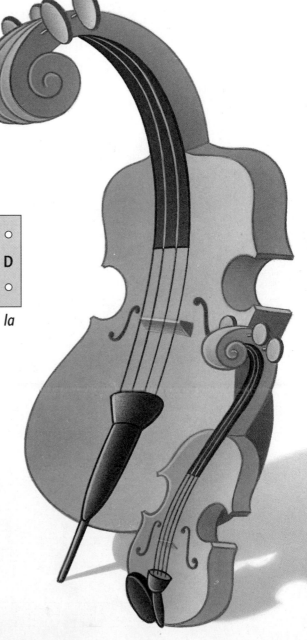

Write

Many folk songs are based on everyday events. Write about an everyday event that might make a good folk song.

VOICES FROM THE HEART

Many Native American songs celebrate the events of everyday life. They also remind people to respect one another and the things of nature. The songs praise what is important in the hearts of the people and in their culture. Listen to songs from the Hopi, the Santa Clara Pueblo, and the Lakota Nations.

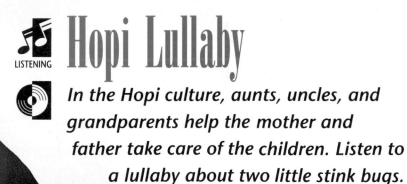

Hopi Lullaby

In the Hopi culture, aunts, uncles, and grandparents help the mother and father take care of the children. Listen to a lullaby about two little stink bugs.

Pueblo Corn Grinding Song

Corn is an important crop among the Pueblo groups. Listen to a song that women from Santa Clara Pueblo sing while they grind corn.

128

Lakota Honor Song

LISTENING

Honoring songs are an important part of the Indian tradition. These songs recognize special achievements. People are honored for the help they give the community. Older people are honored for the useful experience they can pass on. This song honors all Lakotas who fought for the United States.

DESCRIBE the voice of the singer. Is it high or low?

Mohawk basket

dress moccasins

VISUAL ARTS

Traditionally, Native Americans made many of their everyday objects. Hopi women, for example, made beautiful pottery and baskets that were used as trays, serving platters, and containers for corn.

Hopi pottery

Lakota woman's traditional buckskin dress

Modern Native American artists often combine traditional Indian art with other forms of art. Sculptors carve figures and other objects from stone or other materials. Other artists paint pictures.

Oscar Howe, a Lakota, was a painter. Sometimes he used traditional Native American dances in his work. In *Dance of the Double Woman,* he used many shapes and colors.

Stanley Hill, a Mohawk, is famous for his moose antler carvings. The eagle is respected by many Native Americans.

ALPHABET
Stew

Words can be stuffy, as sticky as glue,
but words can be tutored to tickle you too,
to rumble and tumble and tingle and sing,
to buzz like a bumblebee, coil like a spring.

Juggle their letters and jumble their sounds,
swirl them in circles and stack them in mounds,
twist them and tease them and turn them about,
teach them to dance upside down, inside out.

Make mighty words whisper and tiny words roar
in ways no one ever had thought of before;
cook an improbable alphabet stew,
and words will reveal little secrets to you.

—*Jack Prelutsky*

THAT SING

SIMPLY SILLY STORY SONGS

SING this silly story song as you tap with the beat.

FROG WENT A-COURTIN'

Kentucky Folk Song
Additional Words by MMH

Verse

Dm

1. Frog went a-court-in' and he did ride.
(2.) rode right ___ to ___ Miss Mous-ie's ride door,
(3.) took Miss ___ Mous-ie on his knee,
(4.) out my ___ Un-cle Rat's con-sent,
5. Un-cle Rat ___ laughed ___ and shook his sides,

G   F   G

Rink-tum bod-y min-chy cam-bo.

Dm

Sword and buck-ler by his side,
Found Miss Mous-ie sweep-in' the floor.
And said, "Miss Mous-ie, will you mar-ry me?"
I could not mar-ry the pres-i-dent."
To think his niece would be a bride.

Rink - tum bod - y min - chy cam - bo.

Refrain

Ki - man-ee - ro down to Cai - ro, Ki - man-ee - ro Cai - ro.

Shad-dle - ad - dle - ad - a - ba - ba, lad - da - ba - ba link - tum.

Rink - tum bod - y min - chy cam - bo.

2. He
3. He
4. "With -

6. Who will make the wedding gown?
Old Miss Rat from Pumpkin Town.

7. Where will the wedding supper be?
Way down yonder in a hollow tree.

8. What will the wedding supper be?
A fried mosquito and a black-eyed pea.

9. First to come was a bumblebee,
He set his fiddle on his knee.

10. Next to come was a doodle bug,
Carrying a water jug.

11. Next to come was a flying moth;
She laid out the tablecloth.

12. Next to come was an itty-bitty flea
To dance a jig for the bumblebee.

13. Next to come was a big old cow;
She wanted to dance but she
didn't know how.

14. Next to come was a big black snake;
He ate up all the wedding cake.

15. Last to come was an old gray cat;
She swallowed up the mouse and
ate up the rat.

16. Mr. Frog went hopping over the
brook;
A duck came along and swallowed
him up.

17. Now is the end of him and her;
Guess there won't be no
tadpoles covered with fur!

18. Little piece of cornbread lying on
the shelf,
If you want any more you can sing
it yourself!

What sound wakes you up in the morning? In the country, you might wake up to the sound of a rooster's crow.

SING this morning song.

I'LL RISE WHEN
THE ROOSTER CROWS

Appalachian Folk Song
As Sung by Uncle Dave Macon

I'll rise when the rooster crows.
I'll rise when the rooster crows.
I'm going down south where
  the sun shines hot,
Down where the sugarcane grows.

SAY this rooster call four times as others sing the song.

One,	two,	cock-a-	doo- dle	doo!

In music, a pattern that repeats over and over is called an **ostinato.**

"Biddy, Biddy" comes from the warm island of Jamaica. Some words in the song tell about a game. Some words are simply nonsense.

SAY the words in "Biddy, Biddy" as you pat with the beat. On which beats are there four sounds? What are the words on these beats?

Biddy, Biddy

Jamaican Game Song

Biddy, Biddy, hol' fas' los' my gold ring,
Carry me to London, come back again.
Biddy, Biddy, hol' fas' los' my gold ring,
Carry me to London, come back again.

Phrase Your Ideas

This American folk song tells about farm life. Farmers try to reuse the materials that their farms produce so that nothing is wasted.

READ "The Old Sow's Hide," a song from America's past, and find what this farmer reused.

The Old Sow's Hide

American Folk Song

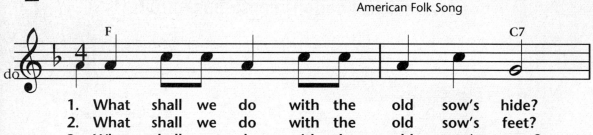

1. What shall we do with the old sow's hide?
2. What shall we do with the old sow's feet?
3. What shall we do with the old sow's meat?
4. What shall we do with the old sow's tail?

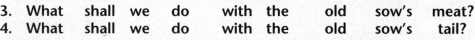

Make a good cush - ion as ev - er did ride.
Make a good pick - les as ev - er was eat.
Make a good ba - con as ev - er was eat.
Make a good whip ___ as ev - er did sail.

When you create
a story, you put words and thoughts
into sentences. When you create music,
you put musical thoughts into musical sentences
called phrases. A **phrase** expresses a complete
musical idea. How many phrases are there in
"The Old Sow's Hide"?

In the movie *The Wizard of Oz,* a young girl named Dorothy finds herself in a strange land. Only a great wizard can help her get home to Kansas. This song is sung as she sets off to find the wizard.

The curved lines above the music show the phrases.

WE'RE OFF TO SEE THE WIZARD

Words by E.Y. Harburg
Music by Harold Arlen

Fol-low the yel-low brick road, ___ Fol-low the yel-low brick road, ___

Fol-low, fol-low, fol-low, fol-low, fol-low the yel-low brick road. ___

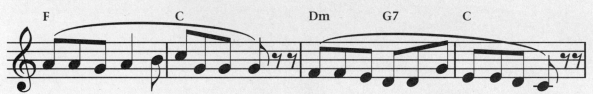

Fol-low the rain-bow o-ver the stream, Fol-low the fel-low who fol-lows a dream.

Fol - low, fol - low, fol - low, fol - low, fol-low the yel-low brick road.

We're off to see the Wiz-ard, ___ The won-der-ful Wiz-ard of Oz. ___

IMAGINE you're on the yellow brick road as you trace the phrases in this song.

We hear he is a whiz of a wiz if ev-er a wiz there was. ___

If ev-er, oh, ev-er a wiz there was, The Wiz-ard of Oz is one be-coz,

be - coz, be-coz, be - coz, be-coz, be - coz, _____

Be - coz of the won-der-ful things he does.

We're off to see the Wiz-ard, __ The won-der-ful Wiz-ard of Oz. __

Notes that Step, Skip, and Repeat

When a melody moves, it can:

- **Step** higher or lower to the next pitch.
- **Skip** higher or lower over one or more pitches.
- **Repeat** on the same pitch.

The pitches in the melody of "Goin' to Ride Up in the Chariot" move by stepping, skipping, and repeating.

LISTEN to "Goin' to Ride Up in the Chariot" and find two wide skips.

Some people think of the chariot ride as a way of traveling to a better life.

Goin' to Ride Up in the Chariot

African American Spiritual

Goin' to ride up in the char - iot soon-er in the morn - ing.,
Soon-er in the morn-ing, Soon-er in the morn-ing. Ride up in the char-iot
Soon-er in the morn-ing, and I hope I'll join the band.

FISHING FOR SKIPS

This song is sometimes sung as people pull ropes and raise sails on fishing boats. The rhythm of the song helps them work together.

FIND the largest skip in this melody.

WANG Ü GER
CHINESE FISHING SONG

Chinese Folk Song
Collected and Transcribed
by Kathy B. Sorensen
English Version by MMH

Mandarin: 白　浪　滔　滔　我　不　怕
Pronunciation: bai　lang　tau　tau　wɔ　bu　pa
English: **Though the waves ___ run ___ high and deep,**

掌　穩　舵　兒　往　前　划
jang　wɛn　duɔ　ər　wang　chiɛn　hwa
We sail on ___ the ___ course we keep.

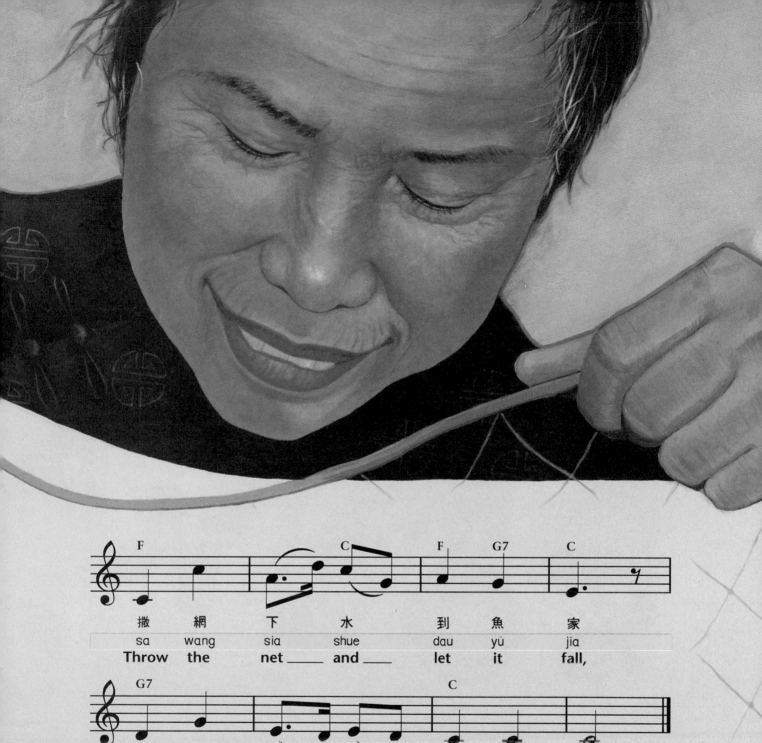

撒　網　　下　水　　到　魚　家
sa　wang　　sia　shue　　dau　yü　jia
Throw　the　　net ___ and ___　let　it　fall,

捕　條　　大　魚　　笑　哈　哈
bu　tiau　　da　yü　　siau　ha　ha
Catch　the　　big - gest ___ fish　of　all.

Four Sounds to a BEAT

One part of the rooster's call, *cockadoodle,* has four sounds to a beat.

Cock-   a-   doo-   dle

In music, four sounds to a beat can look like this:

or this:

These are called **sixteenth notes.**

You can figure out a song you know from its rhythm.

CHOOSE a rhythm that matches the words *one, two, cockadoodle-doo!*

MATCH each word phrase to a rhythm above.

- *Rinktum body minchy cambo*
- *Biddy, Biddy, hol' fas' los' my gold ring*
- *Sooner in the morning, Sooner in the morning*

LISTENING

Overture to *The Marriage of Figaro*

by Wolfgang Amadeus Mozart

The quick rhythms (♪♪♪♪), musical phrases, and tone colors combine to make this music very exciting.

LISTEN to this overture by Mozart. Stand when you hear this pattern.

SPOTLIGHT ON Wolfgang Amadeus

MOZART

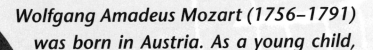

Wolfgang Amadeus Mozart (1756–1791) was born in Austria. As a young child, he could play the piano perfectly. By the time he was five years old, he was already writing music. He and his sister traveled all over Europe performing for kings and queens. Mozart is considered one of the greatest musical geniuses who ever lived. However, during his lifetime, not everyone liked his music. Once, after hearing a piece by Mozart, a king said that Mozart wrote "too many notes." What do you think?

Mozart used many  rhythms. This song, about a colorful market in Australia, also uses many rhythms. Every Saturday, people gather at Salamanca Market to shop for food and crafts.

READ the rhythms in "Salamanca Market."

Say *cockadoodle* for rooster for and *hen* for

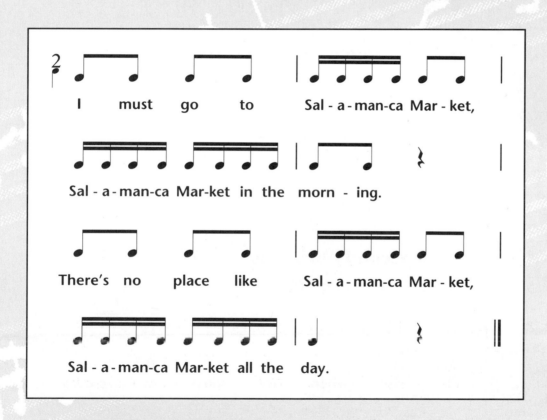

I must go to Sal-a-man-ca Mar-ket,

Sal-a-man-ca Mar-ket in the morn-ing.

There's no place like Sal-a-man-ca Mar-ket,

Sal-a-man-ca Mar-ket all the day.

THINK IT THROUGH

Choose the name of a place. Sing "Salamanca Market" with the name you chose instead of the words *Salamanca Market*. Which way do you like the song better? Why?

do SING IT HIGH

You can learn to read songs with *do* in many different places.

Find *do* on this staff. It's on a ledger line.

do   re   mi   so   la

SING the first phrase of "I'll Rise When the Rooster Crows" using pitch syllables.

do	mi	so	so	so	mi	so
I'll	rise	when	the	roost	- er	crows.

SING the second phrase using pitch syllables and hum when you see "?"

so	la	?	?	?	la	so
I'll	rise	when	the	roost	- er	crows.

Are the "?" pitches higher or lower than *la*?

This highest pitch is called *high do* or *do¹*.

Listen to the song and stand when you hear *do¹*.

150

SING IT LOW

I'll Rise When the Rooster Crows

Appalachian
Folk Song
As Sung by
Uncle Dave Macon

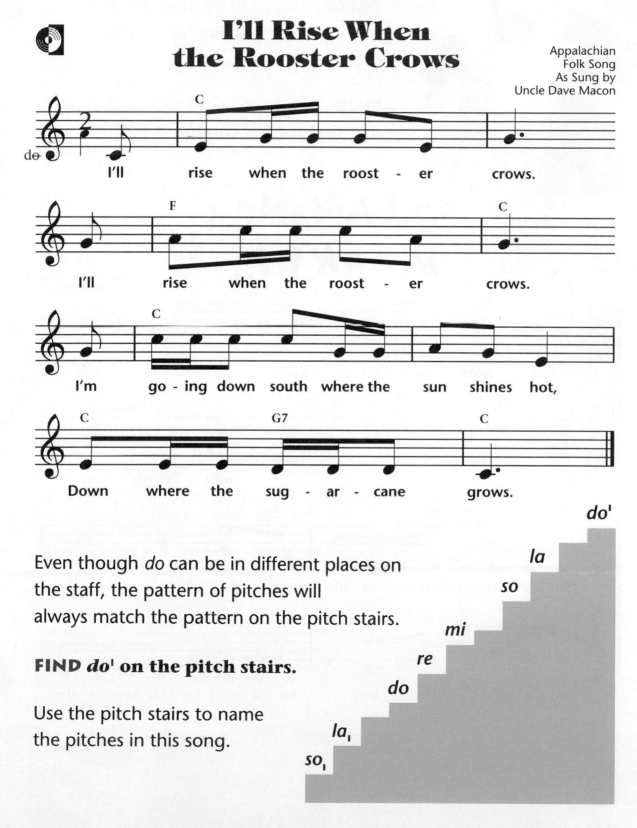

I'll rise when the roost-er crows.

I'll rise when the roost-er crows.

I'm go-ing down south where the sun shines hot,

Down where the sug-ar-cane grows.

Even though *do* can be in different places on the staff, the pattern of pitches will always match the pattern on the pitch stairs.

FIND *do'* on the pitch stairs.

Use the pitch stairs to name the pitches in this song.

You can read all of the rhythms and pitches–including high *do*–in this marketplace song.

FIND each high *do* in the melody of "Salamanca Market."

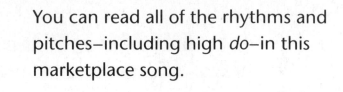
SALAMANCA MARKET

Words and Music
by Mary Goetze

do ·
I must go to Sal - a - man - ca Mar - ket,

do ·
I must go to

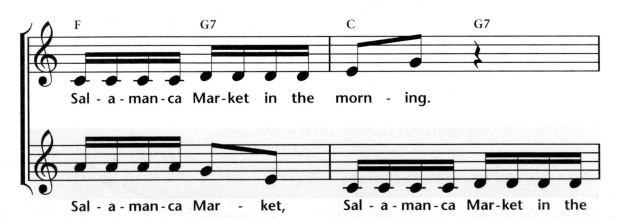

Sal - a - man - ca Mar-ket in the morn - ing.

Sal - a - man - ca Mar - ket, Sal - a - man - ca Mar-ket in the

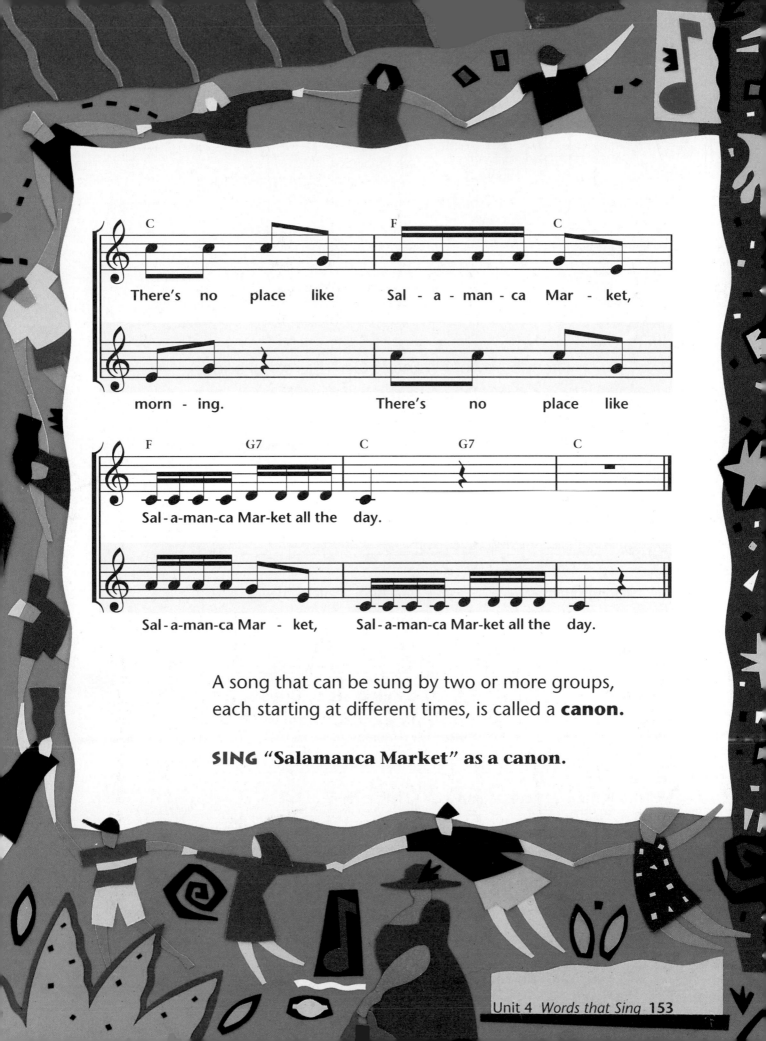

There's no place like Sal-a-man-ca Mar-ket, morn-ing. There's no place like

Sal-a-man-ca Mar-ket all the day.

Sal-a-man-ca Mar-ket, Sal-a-man-ca Mar-ket all the day.

A song that can be sung by two or more groups, each starting at different times, is called a **canon.**

SING "Salamanca Market" as a canon.

The melody of "Wang Ü Ger" has small and large skips. Where is the largest skip?

READ the first two lines of this song with pitch syllables.

Though the waves __ run __ high and deep,

We sail on __ the __ course we keep.

Throw the net __ and __ let it fall,

Catch the big - gest __ fish of all.

MELODY!

**FIND the "?" on the pitch stairs.
What is the name of the new pitch?**

Use the pitch stairs to
name the pitches used
in "Wang Ü Ger."

?'
do'
la
so
mi
re
do

Songs that use *do re mi so* and *la* have a special name.
The name uses the word *penta,* which is Greek for "five."

Make new words using the prefix "penta," or
create something imaginary.

unicorn

pentacorn

"Wang Ü Ger" has five pitches, so you can call this song **pentatonic.**

–*penta* (meaning five)
–*tonic* (meaning pitch)

Why is "Salamanca Market" a pentatonic song?

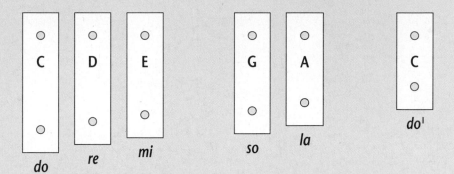

C	D	E		G	A		C
do	*re*	*mi*		*so*	*la*		*do*¹

A **scale** is a group of pitches in order from lowest to highest.

SING the pitch syllables used in "Salamanca Market" in order from lowest to highest.

You just sang a **pentatonic scale!**

PLAY this scale before you sing "Salamanca Market."

do re mi   so la do'   la so mi re   do

MUSICAL CONVERSATIONS

READ this poem to find out how
the animals answer the questions.

The Secret Song

Who saw the petals
 drop from the rose?
I, said the spider,
But nobody knows.

Who saw the sunset
 flash on a bird?
I, said the fish,
But nobody heard.

Who saw the fog
 come over the sea?
I, said the sea pigeon,
Only me.

Who saw the first
 green light of the sun?
I, said the night owl,
The only one.

Who saw the moss
 creep over the stone?
I, said the grey fox,
All alone.

— Margaret Wise Brown

In music, some phrases are like questions, and some are like answers.

CLAP this musical question, and pat this musical answer.

What shall we do with the old sow's hide?

Make a good cush-ion as ev - er did ride.

Try clapping this question and answer with a friend.

How are the phrases alike?

How are they different?

CLAP this question.

CREATE an answer by doing one of the following:

- Move the sixteenth notes to a new place.
- Add a rest for one or more beats.
- Make up a new rhythm for the last four beats.

Music played before a song starts is called an **introduction.** Music added to the end of a song is called a **coda.** The Italian word *coda* means "tail."

PERFORM the questions and answers you just created as an introduction and coda for "Biddy, Biddy."

BIDDY, BIDDY

Jamaican Game Song

Bid - dy, Bid - dy, hol' fas' los' my gold ring,

Car - ry me to Lon - don, come back a - gain.

Bid - dy, Bid - dy, hol' fas' los' my gold ring,

Car - ry me to Lon - don, come back a - gain.

FORM YOUR IDEAS

Just as you can combine sentences to make a paragraph, you can combine musical phrases to create a section of music. The three lines below make up the first section of "Goin' to Ride Up in the Chariot."

Goin' to Ride Up in the Chariot

African American Spiritual

A
Goin' to ride up in the char-iot soon-er in the morn-ing,

Soon-er in the morn-ing, Soon-er in the morn-ing. Ride up in the char-iot

Soon-er in the morn-ing, and I hope I'll join the band.

You can put sections of music together to create a longer song. Add this section to "Goin' to Ride Up in the Chariot."

Oh, Lord, have mer-cy on me, Oh, Lord, have mer-cy on me,

Oh, Lord, have mer-cy on me, and I hope I'll join the band.

Now the song has two sections. Label these sections with the letters *A* and *B*.

SING the song in this order: first section, second section, first section. How would you use the letters *A* and *B* to label this form?

DESIGN IN MUSIC: MEET THE RONDO!

Sections of music can be combined to make a long piece of music. A **rondo** is a long piece of music in which one section always returns. The sections in between are different.

LABEL these instruments with the letters *A*, *B*, and *C*.

vihuela

guitarrón

guitar

Each section of "Los mariachis" has a different melody and a different dance step.

LISTEN to "Los mariachis" and pat with the beat each time you hear the A section.

LISTENING

Los mariachis Mexican Folk Music

"Los mariachis" is performed by a mariachi band. Which instrument plays the melody in the A section?

violin

trumpets

WORDS FOR THE WIZARD

Pretend you are lost in the land of Oz. The Wizard will grant your wish to go home if you can match these word phrases to the pictures.

- Rinktum body minchy cambo
- Make a good cushion
- Follow, follow, follow, follow,
- rise when the rooster crows
- There's no place like

CHECK IT OUT

1. On which beat do you hear four sixteenth notes?

     a. one   **b.** two   **c.** one   **d.** two

2. Choose the rhythm you hear.

     a.

     b.

     c.

     d.

3. How many phrases do you hear?

     a. two   **b.** three   **c.** four   **d.** more than four

4. Which pitches do you hear?

     a.    **c.**

     b.    **d.**

5. Choose the example you hear.

     a.    **c.**

     b.    **d.**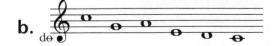

 **C**REATE

Write a Musical Background

CREATE an eight-beat rhythm pattern.
Draw these lines on a piece of paper.

 ___ ___ | ___ ___ | ___ ___ | ___ ___ ||

Write one of these on each line.

With a partner, put your rhythms together to make
a sixteen-beat rhythm pattern. Decide how to play your
rhythm on the two bells *do* (C) and *do'* (C').

do do'

PLAY your piece while someone else
sings one of these songs.

- "The Old Sow's Hide"
- "Salamanca Market"
- "I'll Rise When the Rooster Crows"

Write

Pretend you are lost in
the land of Oz. Write
a letter to the Wizard
explaining why
you want to
go home.

ENCORE
FIT AS A FIDDLE

The fiddle was one of the most popular instruments in colonial America. It was easy to carry and was made by hand. Colonists enjoyed playing songs and dances on the fiddle.

LISTENING

Doubtful Shepherd *English Dance Tune*

An evening gathering of friends in colonial times often ended with dancing. "Doubtful Shepherd" is a short dance that the New England colonists enjoyed.

LISTEN to the sound of the fiddle in this music.

Try this dance yourself. Line up as shown in the picture. The arrows show you how to begin. First, girls hold hands and walk a pathway behind boys. Then, boys hold hands and walk behind girls.

The violin is sometimes called a fiddle, but violin music sounds very different from fiddle music. The beautiful sound of the violin makes it a very important part of the orchestra. It is the smallest and highest-sounding member of the string family.

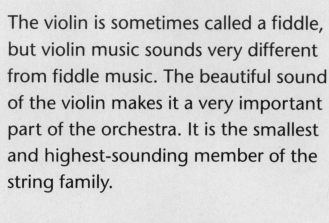

LISTENING

Waltz of the Flowers

from The Nutcracker by Peter Tchaikovsky

LISTEN to the "Waltz of the Flowers." The violins are playing the melody.

THE STRING FAMILY

violin   viola   violoncello   double bass

LISTENING

Grasshoppers Three

by Henry Newbolt
adapted by Ruth Boshkoff

The fiddle is a very popular instrument. Many stories and songs have been told about it. The song "Grasshoppers Three" tells the story of three fun-loving grasshoppers who fiddled, danced, and sang.

Work, Play

and Sing!

They Were My People

They were those who cut cane
to the rhythm of the sunbeat.

They were those who carried cane
to the rhythm of the sunbeat.

They were those who crushed cane
to the rhythm of the sunbeat.

They were women weeding, carrying babies
to the rhythm of the sunbeat.

They were my people working so hard
to the rhythm of the sunbeat.

They were my people, working so hard
to the rhythm of the sunbeat—long ago
to the rhythm of the sunbeat.

—Grace Nichols

SONGS FOR WORK

People everywhere create songs for working and playing. This game song comes from the Maori people in New Zealand. In the Maori language, *tititorea* means "little sticks." Some Maori people sing this song as they play a game with the sticks.

LISTEN to "Tititorea" as you perform this movement. Say "Floor, tap, out."

1. Tap floor.

AND PLAY

2. Tap sticks together.

3. Move sticks apart.

The beats in "Tititorea" are grouped in sets of three. The first beat in each set is the strong beat, or downbeat. Try a different movement to show the strong beats.

LISTEN to "Tititorea" again and tap the floor on Beat 1. Freeze on Beats 2 and 3.

Workers sing "One, Two, Three!" as they
work in the cane fields in Barbados.

CREATE a four-beat movement ostinato for
"One, Two, Three!" Use a heavier movement
on the downbeat.

One, Two, Three!

Words and Music
by Maurice Gardner
In the style of a Barbados Work Song

1.–4. One,   two,   three!

{ Cut down de sug - ar cane all   day.
{ Bun - dle de sug - ar cane all   day.
{ Load up   de sug - ar truck all   day.
{ Walk down de mar - ket road all   day.

One,   two,   three!

{ Cut down de sug - ar cane all   day.
{ Bun - dle de sug - ar cane all   day.
{ Load up   de sug - ar truck all   day.
{ Walk down de mar - ket road all   day.

One,   two,   three!

{ Cut down de sug - ar cane all   day.
{ Bun - dle de sug - ar cane all   day.
{ Load up   de sug - ar truck all   day.
{ Walk down de mar - ket road all   day.

Gm — **F** — **C7** — **F**

Work all de day-o, work all de day-o,
{
Cut down de sug-ar cane all day.
Bun-dle de sug-ar cane all day.
Load up de sug-ar truck all day.
Walk down de mar-ket road all day.
}

Gm — **F** — **C7** — **F**

Work all de day-o, work all de day-o,
{
cut down de sug-ar cane.
bun-dle de sug-ar cane.
load up de sug-ar truck.
walk down de mar-ket road.
}

LISTENING

Cuequita de los Coyas

Andean Highlands Folk Music

The Coyas people come from the Andes Mountains in South America. They dance to this colorful native flute music. Cuequita de los Coyas *means "Dance of the Coyas."*

CHOOSE the beat grouping that matches "Cuequita de los Coyas."

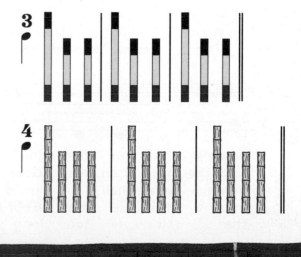

AN UPBEAT JOKE!

Do you think this is a song for work or a song for play? Why?

There's a Hole in the Bucket

American Dialogue Song
Traditional German Melody "Liebe Heinrich"

1. There's a hole in the buck-et, dear Li-za, dear Li-za,
2. Mend the hole, then, dear Geor-gie, dear Geor-gie, dear Geor-gie,
3. With ___ what shall I mend it, dear Li-za, dear Li-za,
4. With a straw, ___ dear Geor-gie, dear Geor-gie, dear Geor-gie,
5. The ___ straw is too long, ___ dear Li-za, dear Li-za,

There's a hole in the buck-et, dear Li-za, a hole.
Mend the hole, then, dear Geor-gie, dear Geor-gie, the hole.
With ___ what shall I mend it, dear Li-za, with what?
With a straw, ___ dear Geor-gie, dear Geor-gie, a straw.
The ___ straw is too long, ___ dear Li-za, too long.

180

6. Cut the straw, dear Georgie,
   dear Georgie, dear Georgie,
   Cut the straw, dear Georgie,
   dear Georgie, the straw.

7. With what shall I cut it,
   dear Liza, . . . with what?

8. With a knife, dear Georgie,
   . . . a knife.

9. The knife is too dull,
   dear Liza, . . . too dull.

10. Then sharpen it, dear Georgie,
    . . . then sharpen it.

11. With what shall I sharpen it,
    dear Liza, . . . with what?

12. With a stone, dear Georgie,
    . . . a stone.

13. The stone is too dry,
    dear Liza, . . . too dry.

14. Then wet it, dear Georgie,
    . . . then wet it.

15. With what shall I wet it,
    dear Liza, . . . with what?

16. With water, dear Georgie,
    . . . with water.

17. In what shall I get it,
    dear Liza, . . . in what?

18. In a bucket, dear Georgie,
    . . . in a bucket.

19. There's a hole in the bucket,
    dear Liza, . . . a hole.

How many phrases are in each verse?

AN UPBEAT PHRASE!

PAT, clap, and snap as you sing "There's a Hole in the Bucket."

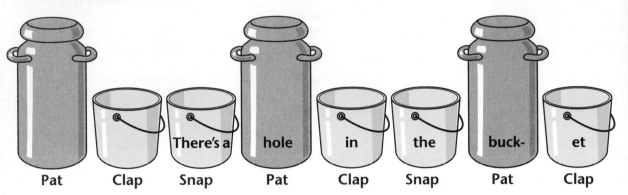

Pat   Clap   Snap   Pat   Clap   Snap   Pat   Clap

Do the phrases begin on Beat 1, 2, or 3?

When a phrase starts before the first downbeat, it starts on an upbeat.

This Creole lullaby is from Louisiana.
The Creole culture is a mix of French,
Spanish, and African traditions.

Sweep, Sweep Away
Creole Folk Song

Sweep, sweep, sweep away,

Sweep the road of dreams,

People say that, in the night,

The turtle will talk, it seems.

The turtle will talk, it seems.

Which phrases begin on Beat 1, the
downbeat? The upbeat?

Singing with Added Sounds

A lullaby like "Sweep, Sweep Away" is usually sung by one person, without any other musical sounds. Some songs are sung with **accompaniment,** or other musical sounds added to them.

LISTEN to the accompaniment in "Sandy Land."

No Accompaniment

Accompaniment

You can add your own accompaniment to "Sandy Land."

SING "Sandy Land," snapping on the words in blue and patting on the words in red.

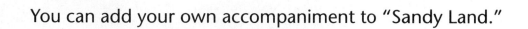 # Sandy Land Texas Folk Song

1. I make my living in the sandy land,
   I make my living in the sandy land,
   I make my living in the sandy land,
   Oh ladies, fare you well.

2. They raise big taters in the sandy land,
   They raise big taters in the sandy land,
   They raise big taters in the sandy land,
   Oh ladies, fare you well.

3. Sift the meal and save the bran,
   Sift the meal and save the bran,
   Sift the meal and save the bran,
   Oh ladies, fare you well.

4. One more river I'm bound to cross,
   One more river I'm bound to cross,
   One more river I'm bound to cross,
   Oh ladies, fare you well.

LISTEN to "Sandy Land" and move with a friend when you hear the accompaniment. Freeze when you hear only singing.

The guitar is used by many people to accompany songs. Why do you think the guitar is so popular?

meet Sally Rogers

Sally Rogers is a strong believer in saving our planet and creating world peace. She writes many songs with these themes. If you went to one of her concerts, you'd hear her clear soprano voice and see her play stringed instruments, including a guitar, banjo, and an Appalachian dulcimer. In her warm and friendly way, she'd invite you to sing along!

THINK IT THROUGH

What other musical instruments could you play to accompany "Sandy Land"? Why would these instruments make a good accompaniment?

ACCOMPANIMENT WITH CHORDS

Some accompaniments are made up of chords. A **chord** is made when three or more pitches are sounded together. Instruments such as guitars, pianos, autoharps, or bells can produce chords. Line up the bells like the pictures below and take turns playing these chords.

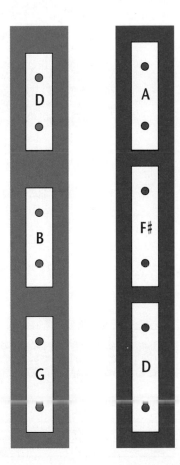

CHOOSE one bell from either the red set or the blue set. Play the bell as you sing the song on page 185.

You can also make a chord with voices. How could singers make a chord?

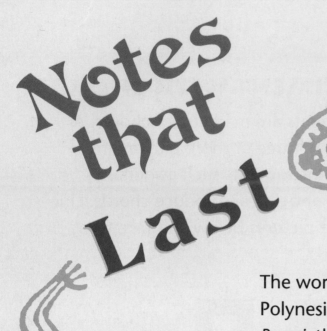

Notes that Last

The words in "Tititorea" tell an old Polynesian story. They tell how sad *Rangi,* the sky, is to be apart from *Papa,* the earth. The Maori people sing this song as they perform the stick game.

PLAY the Maori stick game on page 176 to accompany "Tititorea."

PLAY the Maori stick game on page 176 to accompany "Tititorea."

TITITOREA

MAORI STICK GAME

New Zealand Folk Song
Collected and Transcribed
by Kathy B. Sorensen

Maori: **E hi - ne ho - ki mai ra.**
Pronunciation: e hi ne ho ki maı ɾa

E pa - pa___ wai - a - ri ta - ku nei___ ma - hi,
e pa pa waı a ɾi ta ku neı ma hi

ta - ku nei __ ma - hi tu - ku roi - ma ta. Au
ta ku nei ma hi tu ku ɾɔɪ ma ta au

e - au - e _____ ka - ma - te au,
e au e ka ma te au

Go back to the beginning and sing to the end
(Da Capo al Fine)

E hi - ne ho - ki mai ra.
e hi ne ho ki maɪ ɾa

DOTTED HALF NOTES

What does the meter sign $\begin{smallmatrix}3\\4\end{smallmatrix}$ tell you?

Find the 𝅗𝅥. in "Tititorea." Then tap on the symbols below as you listen to "Tititorea."

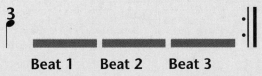

Beat 1   Beat 2   Beat 3

Trace the line when you hear a 𝅗𝅥.

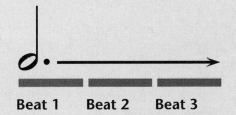

Beat 1   Beat 2   Beat 3

A **dotted half note** (𝅗𝅥.) lasts three beats. How many dotted half notes are in "Tititorea"?

When you watch a sunset, you can have many different feelings. What words in the first verse of this song tell you how this person is feeling?

EVERY NIGHT

Appalachian Folk Song

1. Ev' - ry night when the sun goes __ in,
(2.) love don't weep, true __ love don't __ mourn.
(3.) wish to the Lord, that __ train would __ come.

ev' - ry night when the sun goes in,
True love don't weep, true __ love don't mourn.
I wish to the Lord, that __ train would come.

ev' - ry night when the sun goes __ in,
True love don't weep, true __ love don't __ mourn.
I wish to the Lord, that __ train would __ come.

I hang down my head and mourn-ful __ cry. 2. True
I'm go - ing a - way to Mar - ble __ Town. 3. I
And take ____ me back where I come __ from.

In $\frac{4}{4}$ meter, a sound that lasts a whole measure, or four beats, is called a **whole note.** A silence that lasts a whole measure is called a **whole rest** (━).

TAP **this ostinato as you listen to "Every Night."**

"Sweep, Sweep Away" is also in $\frac{4}{4}$ meter. It has four beats in each measure.

FIND the whole note (o) in "Sweep, Sweep Away."
Now find the dotted half notes (𝅗𝅥.).

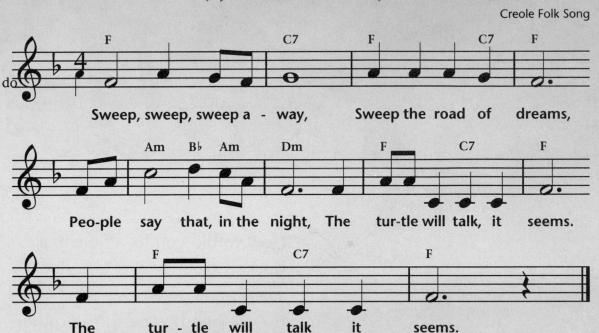

Sweep, Sweep Away

Creole Folk Song

Sweep, sweep, sweep a - way, Sweep the road of dreams,

Peo-ple say that, in the night, The tur-tle will talk, it seems.

The tur - tle will talk it seems.

SING "Sweep, Sweep Away" as you watch the notation. Tap four times when you sing a whole note (o). Tap three times when you sing a dotted half note (𝅗𝅥.).

Snap It Up!

How would you fix a hole in a bucket? Georgie and Liza don't seem to be getting very far. Give them a hand by performing the pat-clap-snap pattern over and over as you sing this song. Start by snapping on the upbeat *There's a . . .*

There's a Hole in the Bucket

American Dialogue Song
Traditional German Melody "Liebe Heinrich"

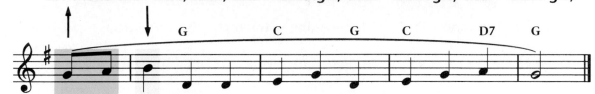

1. There's a hole in the buck-et, dear Li - za, dear Li - za,
2. Mend the hole, then, dear Geor-gie, dear Geor-gie, dear Geor-gie,

There's a hole in the buck-et, dear Li - za, a hole.
Mend the hole, then, dear Geor-gie, dear Geor-gie, the hole.

The arrows show the upbeats and downbeats.

SING these two verses again. Snap-pat only on the arrows.

"There's a Hole in the Bucket" is in $\frac{3}{?}$ meter, but the last measure has only 2 beats. Where's the third beat?

HINT: Perform the song twice, using the pat-clap-snap pattern.

Unit 5 *Work, Play—and Sing!* **193**

Ton moulin
Your Windmill

French Folk Song
English Version by MMH

French: Ton mou - lin, ton mou - lin, ton mou - lin va trop vi - te,
Pronunciation: tɔ̃ mu lɛ̃ tɔ̃ mu lɛ̃ tɔ̃ mu lɛ̃ va tro vi tə
English: Ton mou - lin, ton mou - lin, your ___ mill turns too quick-ly.

Ton mou - lin, ton mou - lin, ton mou - lin va trop fort!
tɔ̃ mu lɛ̃ tɔ̃ mu lɛ̃ tɔ̃ mu lɛ̃ va tro fɔr
Ton mou - lin, ton mou - lin, your ___ mill turns too strong!

Ton mou - lin, ton mou - lin va trop vi - te,
tɔ̃ mu lɛ̃ tɔ̃ mu lɛ̃ va tro vi tə
Ton mou - lin, ton mou - lin turns too quick - ly,

Ton mou - lin, ton mou - lin va trop fort!
tɔ̃ mu lɛ̃ tɔ̃ mu lɛ̃ va tro fɔr
Ton mou - lin, ton mou - lin turns too strong!

Ton mou - lin, ton mou - lin, ton mou - lin va trop vi - te,
tɔ̃ mu lɛ̃ tɔ̃ mu lɛ̃ tɔ̃ mu lɛ̃ va trɔ vi tə
Ton mou - lin, ton mou - lin, your ___ mill turns too quick-ly.

Ton mou - lin, ton mou - lin, ton mou - lin va trop fort!
tɔ̃ mu lɛ̃ tɔ̃ mu lɛ̃ tɔ̃ mu lɛ̃ va trɔ fɔr
Ton mou - lin, ton mou - lin, your ___ mill turns too strong!

Which section of "Ton moulin" begins
on an upbeat? Downbeat?

**PERFORM a dance with each section
of "Ton moulin." Do a millwheel
movement for section A. Choose your
partner and whirl on section B.**

Meter Match

Do you ever make up rhymes when you walk to school or go for a long car ride? Maybe you sing songs or trade tongue twisters with a friend. Try this rhyme. Change *salt and PEPPER* to the silliest food you can think of!

Mabel, Mabel

Mabel, Mabel, set the table, Don't forget the salt and PEPPER!

—*Carl Withers*

CHOOSE one of these items and say the poem again.

- **mustard**
- **lemonade**
- **spoons**
- **red hot pepper**

Mabel's in such a hurry she can't decide
whether to say this poem in $\frac{4}{}$ or $\frac{3}{}$ meter!

SAY "Mabel, Mabel" in $\frac{4}{}$ meter.

Ma - bel, Ma - bel,   set   the   ta - ble.   Don't for - get   the _____ .

SAY "Mabel, Mabel" in $\frac{3}{}$ meter.

Ma - bel, Ma - bel,   set   the ta - ble.   Don't for - get   the _____ .

Which do you like better? Why?

Allemande Tripla

by Johann Hermann Schein

Sometimes composers use both $\frac{3}{2}$ and $\frac{4}{2}$ when they write music. This music was written hundreds of years ago by a German composer named Johann Hermann Schein.

LISTEN to the sounds of recorders and lutes in this music.

THE CONCERT

This group of musicians was painted over 300 years ago by J. van Bijlert. How are these instruments similar to, or different from instruments you see or play today?

"Ton moulin" and "Allemande Tripla" have two things in common. They both change meters, and they both have A and B sections.

LISTENING MAP *Follow the listening map below to find an added section in "Allemande Tripla." What is the letter of this new section? Which sections are in $\frac{4}{4}$? In $\frac{3}{4}$?*

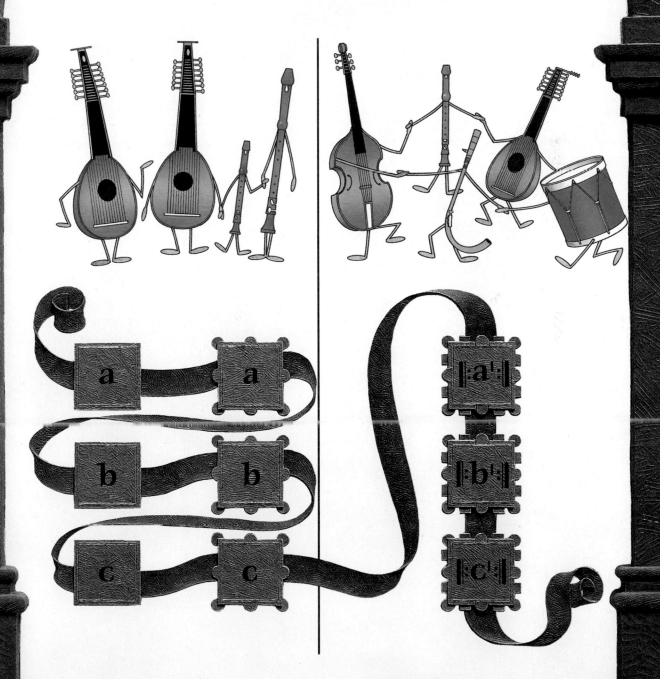

TRADITIONS IN SONG

If you go to the Cattaraugus reservation, in western New York state, you might see this Seneca Stomp Dance.

Senecas are a Native American nation. Senecas perform stomp-dance songs to start a ceremony or an evening of fun. Creek, Seminole, and Cherokee nations also perform stomp dances.

For hundreds of years, people have learned songs by listening to other people perform them. You can learn music this way, too!

LISTEN to "Seneca Stomp Dance" performed by the people of the Seneca nation.

Seneca Stomp Dance

by Avery Jimerson

Ya yo we ye ha, Yo we ya,
(repeat four times)

Ya yo we ye ha, Yo we ya,
We ha yo we ye ha, Yo we ya,
(repeat four times) Yo.

Did you hear a repeated pattern?

PERFORM the stomp-dance movement as you sing the song.

Slide your right foot forward, then "stomp" your left foot next to it.

You can read pitches using pitch syllables. You can also read pitches using letter names. The **treble clef** or **G clef** (𝄞) at the beginning of a staff tells you that the pitch on the second line is G. What are the letter names of the next two pitches?

SING Sandy Land" and play the
tinted pitches (G, A, and B) on bells.

SANDY LAND

Texas Folk Song

1.   I   make   my   liv - ing   in   the   sand - y   land,
2. They   raise   big   ta - ters   in   the   sand - y   land,
3.   Sift   the   meal ___   and ___   save   the   bran,
4.   One   more   riv - er   I'm ___   bound   to   cross,

    I   make   my   liv - ing   in   the   sand - y   land,
They   raise   big   ta - ters   in   the   sand - y   land,
    Sift   the   meal ___   and ___   save   the   bran,
    One   more   riv - er   I'm ___   bound   to   cross,

    I   make   my   liv - ing   in   the   sand - y   land,
They   raise   big   ta - ters   in   the   sand - y   land,
    Sift   the   meal ___   and ___   save   the   bran,
    One   more   riv - er   I'm ___   bound   to   cross,

Oh   la - dies,   fare   you   well.

SHARP CONTRAS

THROUGH-GOING LINE

Wassily Kandinsky used loud colors and shapes with sharp edges to create *Through-going Line,* a painting that is full of explosive energy. What words would you use to describe this painting?

Kunstsammlung Nordrhein-Westfalen

TS

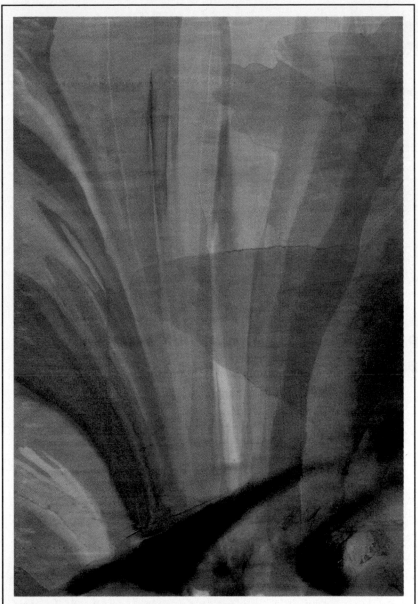

Longitude by Morris Louis, 1954 Acrylic on canvas Courtesy of Ancre Emmerich Gallery, New York

LONGITUDE

Morris Louis used pastel colors and long lines to create *Longitude.* What words would you use to describe this painting?

SING "Every Night" and "One, Two, Three!" Which painting best matches the feeling of each song? Why?

Sometimes a song can have sections that feel very different. The song "Ton moulin" has a middle section that feels different from the first or last section.

PERFORM the movements shown on page 195. Then sing "Ton moulin" to find which section has a (♩.).

PLAY this melodic ostinato on bells during the A sections of "Ton moulin."

G G A A A B

These instruments are used in "Allemande Tripla."

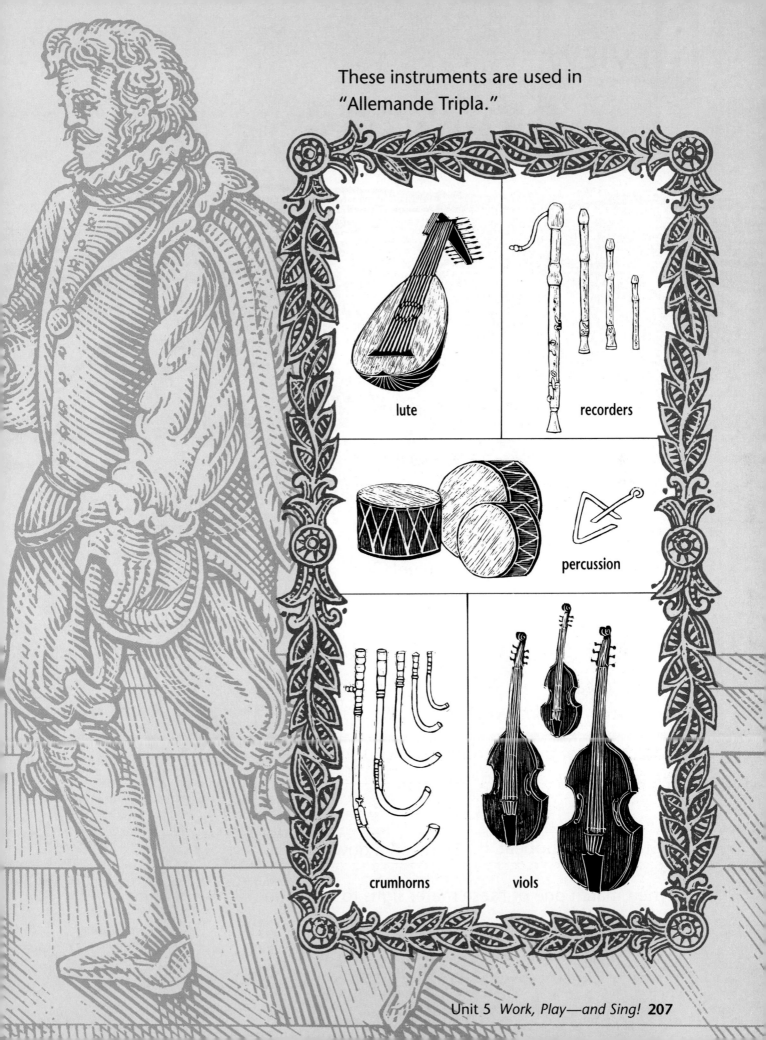

lute

recorders

percussion

crumhorns

viols

 REVIEW

UPBEAT SONGS

Match each song title to a picture. Sing
each song and perform the movements.
Then decide whether the song is for work or play.

- "One, Two, Three"
- "Tititorea"
- "Sweep, Sweep Away"

- "There's a Hole in
  the Bucket"
- "Ton moulin"

Match one of these symbols to each song.

 Starts on an upbeat

 Starts on a downbeat

Then match one of these meter signs to each song.

CHECK IT OUT

1. Which of these melodies has groups of three ($\frac{3}{4}$ meter)?

   a.   **b.**   **c.**

2. Which of these melodies has groups of four ($\frac{4}{4}$ meter)?

   a.   **b.**   **c.**

3. Which of these melodies starts on an upbeat?

   a.   **b.**   **c.**

4. Which of these melodies starts on a downbeat?

   a.   **b.**   **c.**

5. In which measure do you hear the dotted half note?

   a. (measure one) **b.** (measure two) **c.** (measure three) **d.** (measure four)

6. In which measure do you hear the whole note?

   a. (measure one)   **b.** (measure two)   **c.** (measure three)   **d.** (measure four)

7. Which rhythm do you hear?

   a.
   b.
   c.
   d.

210

CREATE

Write Ostinato Accompaniments!

Draw these lines on a piece of paper.

Choose from these rhythms to fill in the measures.

Choose an unpitched instrument, such as a drum.

PLAY your ostinato as an accompaniment to "Cuequita de los Coyas" or "Tititorea."

Repeat these steps to create an ostinato in 4/4 meter. Then play your ostinato as an accompaniment to "Sweep, Sweep Away."

Write

Choose a song to sing with an activity you do every day. Write about why you chose that song.

All About the DOUBLE BASS

The double bass is the largest member of the string family. Do you know the names of the other instruments in this family?

The double bass is the lowest-sounding string instrument. It usually plays a background part, but its rich sound is very important to the orchestra. In jazz bands, the bass is played **pizzicato,** or plucked.

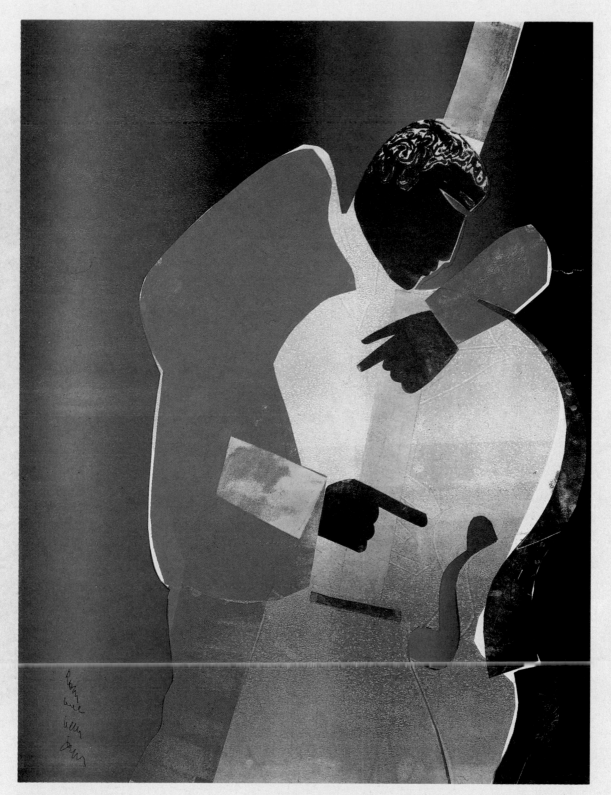

IN E SHARP

This is a collage by Romare Bearden (1914–1988).
A collage is a work of art made by pasting different
materials, such as paper or cloth, together.

MEET *Milt* Hinton

Milt Hinton has played double bass for nearly sixty years. He has appeared with many great jazz artists such as Louis Armstrong, Charlie Parker, and Benny Goodman. During his long career, Hinton has made more records than any other jazz musician. He is also an excellent photographer.

LISTEN to this great double bass player talk about his career.

WRITE about the part of the interview that you found most interesting. Share your essay with the class.

The double bass can be played like a rhythm instrument in a **slap bass** style. Instead of just plucking the notes, the player also slaps the double bass to create these sounds:

Boom CHUK-A **Boom** CHUK-A
Boom CHUK-A **Boom** **Boom**

Can you say these sounds?

SING the following pattern in a slap bass style.

Boom   chuk - a   boom   chuk - a

boom   chuk - a   boom   boom

LISTENING

Three Little Words

from Trio Jeepy by B. Kalmar and H. Ruby

LISTEN to Milt Hinton improvise in a slap bass style.

IDENTIFY a familiar song. Raise your hand when you hear Milt Hinton playing it. What is the name of this song?

THE POSTMAN

The whistling postman swings along.
His bag is deep and wide,
And messages from all the world
Are bundled up inside.

The postman's walking up our street.
Soon now he'll ring my bell.
Perhaps there'll be a letter stamped
In Asia. Who can tell?

—*Anonymous*

WHAT'S THE MESSAGE?

What news have you heard recently? Did you get your news from a letter? Television? Newspaper? Friend?

LISTEN to "I Got a Letter" as you think of getting news that makes you happy.

I Got a Letter

South Carolina
Singing Game

I got a let-ter this morn - ing, Oh, yes;

I got a let-ter this morn - ing, Oh, yes.

Listen to "I Got a Letter" again and guess what kind of news was in each of the four letters. How did the music change to show each different kind of news?

People can express feelings through their paintings.

COMPARE these two paintings.

FIRST DAY OF SCHOOL
Catrin Zipfel, age 10, is from the Federal Republic of Germany.

Courtesy of The U.S. Committee for UNICEF

Courtesy of The U.S. Committee for UNICEF

SAD FAMILY
Jacqueline Menendez Encalade, age 11, is from Ecuador.

During years of slavery, enslaved African Americans sang songs about freedom. Many escaped to freedom by following a secret path north. The chariot in "Good News" stands for a way to travel to freedom.

SING "Good News" to send a message of joy!

GOOD NEWS

African American Spiritual

crescendo

Good news! Char - i - ot's a - com - in',

Good news! Char-i-ot's a-com-in', Good news!

Char-i-ot's a-com-in', and I don't want it to leave me be - hind.

The feelings expressed in a piece of music change with the way it's performed. Musical markings tell you how to perform a song.

SING "Good News" three different ways. How do your feelings change?

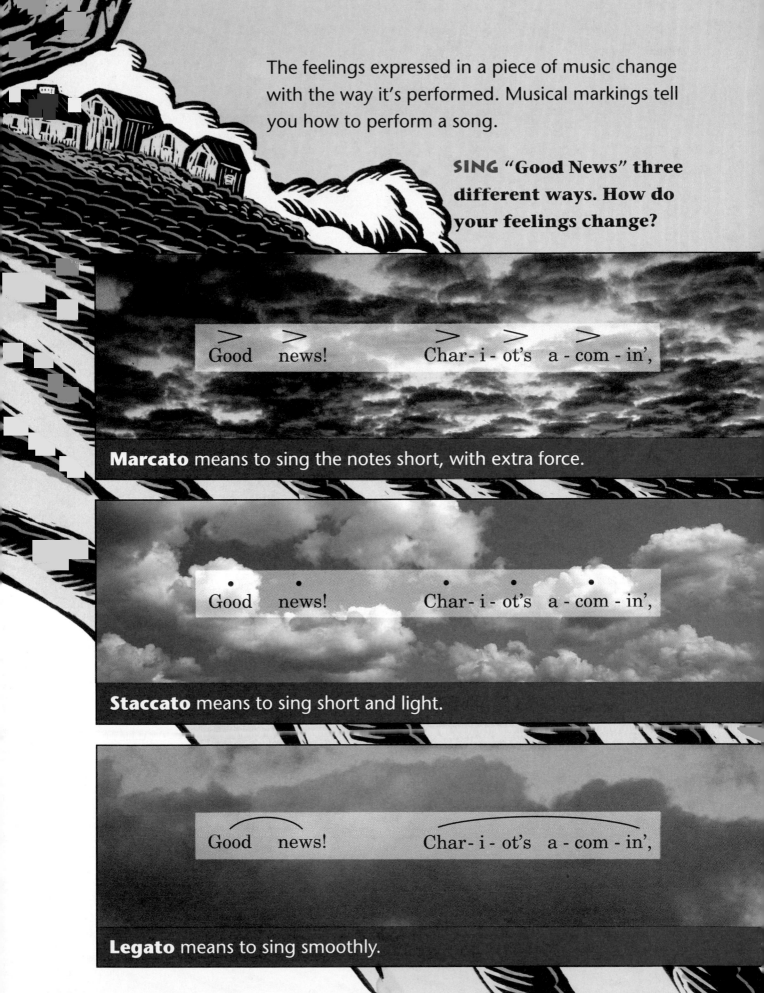

>   >   >   >   >
Good   news!   Char-i-ot's a-com-in',

Marcato means to sing the notes short, with extra force.

Good   news!   Char-i-ot's a-com-in',

Staccato means to sing short and light.

Good   news!   Char-i-ot's a-com-in',

Legato means to sing smoothly.

221

NO BAD

This song is from the Broadway musical *The Wiz*,
based on the story *The Wonderful Wizard of Oz.*

Don't Nobody Bring Me No Bad News

Words and Music by Charlie Smalls

1. If we're go-in' to be bud-dies bet-ter
   talk-in' to ___ me ___ don't be
   mes-sage in your head ___ or in

bone up on the rules. ___ 'Cause don't no-bod-y
cry-in' the blues _____ 'Cause don't no-bod-y
some-thing you can't lose, ___ But don't you ev-er

bring me no bad news. ___ You can be my best of
bring me no bad news. ___ You can verb-al-ize and
bring me no bad news. ___ If you're gon-na bring me

friends as op-posed to pay-in' dues,
vo-cal-ize, but just bring me ___ the clues;
some-thing, bring me some-thing I can use,

NEWS

But don't no-bod-y bring me ___ no bad ___ news. ___
But don't no-bod-y bring me ___ no bad ___ news. ___
But don't you _____ bring me ___ no bad ___ news. ___

Refrain

No bad news, no bad news.

Don't you ev - er bring me no bad news. ___

'Cause I'll make you _ an of-fer, child, _ that you can-not _ re - fuse,

so don't no-bod-y bring me ___ no bad ___ news. ___ 2. When you're
3. Bring some

Don't you bring me ___ no bad news.

HOME, SWEET HOME

"Don't Nobody Bring Me No Bad News" has an ending that sounds very complete, or final. The melody ends on the **tonal center,** or **home tone.** Many melodies start on the home tone, move away from it, and then return. It's often the last pitch of a melody.

Choose a place in your classroom to call home.

MOVE away as you sing "Don't Nobody Bring Me No Bad News." Return home by the end of the song.

LISTENING

March of the Wooden Soldiers

from *Album for the Young*

by Piotr Ilyich Tchaikovsky
arranged by Rostislav Dubinsky

Listen to "March of the Wooden Soldiers" as you pat with the beat.

Listen again, as you march away from your home position. Return home by the end of the final phrase.

224

"Old Man Moses" also ends on the home tone.

LISTEN to the doctor's advice in "Old Man Moses."

Old Man Moses

African American Game Song

Old man Mo - ses, sick in bed, ___

Called for the doc - tor and the doc - tor said, ___

"Please step for - ward and turn a - round, ___

Do the ho - key po - key and get out of town!" ___

SING "Old Man Moses" to find the words sung on the home tone.

Music with Style

Musical style refers to everything used in a piece of music: rhythms, pitches, tone colors, instruments, and accompaniment. Your clothes also have style.

COMPARE the clothes in these three pictures. Which style would you choose to wear?

1920s

1950s

Art has different styles, too. How are these two paintings different?

EDWARD VI, WHEN DUKE OF CORNWALL

Hans Holbein, the court painter, finished this realistic portrait painting in 1543. It shows Edward when he was six years old. He became King of England four years later.

1990s

MARILYN

Andy Warhol finished this silkscreen and oil painting of Marilyn Monroe in 1964.

meet Midori

Performers such as Midori have their own style. When she was your age, she practiced the violin three to four hours a day! At eleven, she made her first appearance with the New York Philharmonic. Midori's mother was also a violinist. Midori remembers being surrounded by music as she grew up in Japan. Now she travels all around the world giving concerts and making recordings. She loves making music and hopes to do this all her life.

LISTENING  **Caprice in A Minor** excerpts

by Niccolò Paganini

"Caprice" was written for the violin about 100 years ago.

LISTENING MAP *Listen to Midori play "Caprice" as you follow this listening map.*

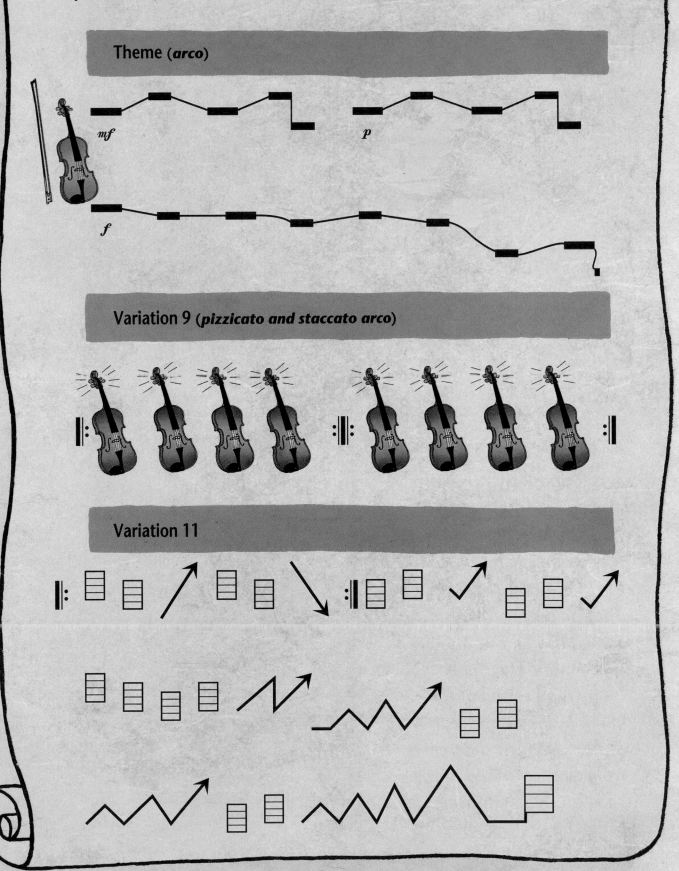

LOOK at these two instruments. Why might they sound different?

violin

Variations excerpts

by Andrew Lloyd Webber

"Variations" was recently written by Andrew Lloyd Webber. It has a more modern musical style than the "Caprice in A Minor." Both pieces start with the same melody, but they don't sound the same.

The high sound of the violin in the "Caprice in A Minor" is much different from the low sound of the cello used in "Variations." How else are the pieces different?

cello

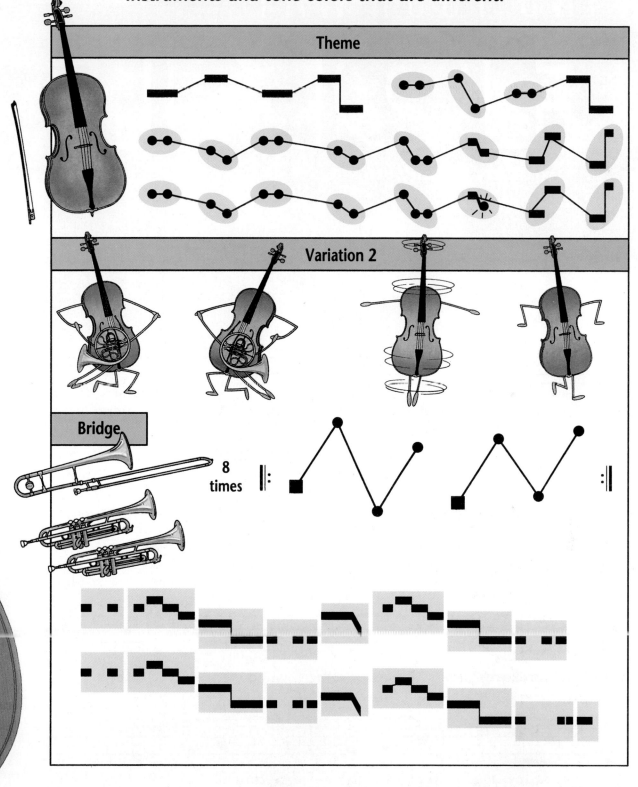

COMPARE the "Caprice in A Minor" with "Variations." Think about the instruments, rhythms, and accompaniment.

FIND YOUR WAY HOME

LISTEN to "Killy Kranky" to find the home tone.

KILLY KRANKY

Appalachian Folk Song
New and Additional
Words and Music
by Jean Ritchie

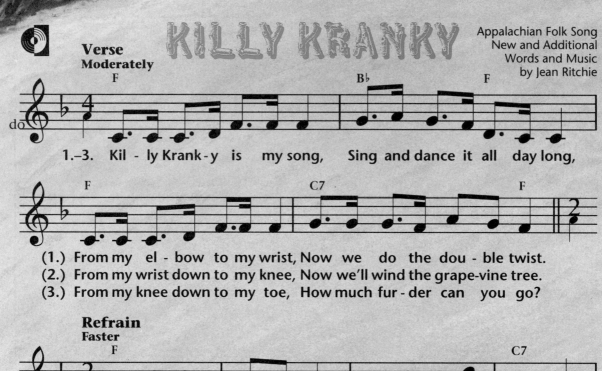

Verse
Moderately

1.–3. Kil - ly Krank - y is my song, Sing and dance it all day long,

(1.) From my el - bow to my wrist, Now we do the dou - ble twist.
(2.) From my wrist down to my knee, Now we'll wind the grape-vine tree.
(3.) From my knee down to my toe, How much fur - der can you go?

Refrain
Faster

Broke my arm, broke my arm, swing-in' pret - ty Nan - cy,

Broke my leg, broke my leg, dan - cin' Kil - ly Krank - y.

The home tone in "Killy Kranky" is *do.* It's in the first space. Which phrase ends on *do*?

"Killy Kranky" is a game song from Appalachia, a mountain area in the southeastern United States.

Meet
JEAN RITCHIE

Jean Ritchie wrote some of the words for "Killy Kranky." She was raised in the Cumberland Mountains of Kentucky. She was the youngest of 14 children. As a child, she "would worry that there would sometimes come an evening when they wouldn't sing!" Her family sang songs from their English, Scottish, and Irish ancestors.

Appalachian dulcimer

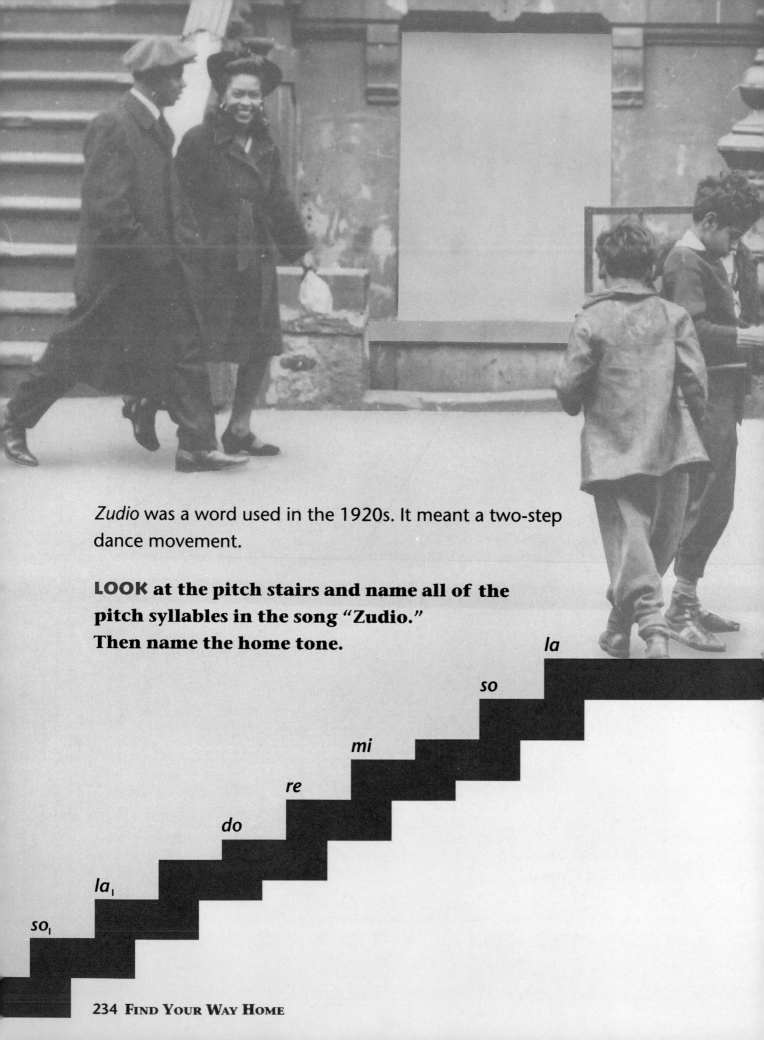

Zudio was a word used in the 1920s. It meant a two-step
dance movement.

LOOK at the pitch stairs and name all of the
pitch syllables in the song "Zudio."
Then name the home tone.

la

so

mi

re

do

la₁

so₁

LISTEN to "Zudio" and hum the home tone.

ZUDIO

Traditional African American Street
Game Adapted by Janet McMillion

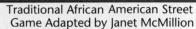

1. Here we go Zu - di-o, Zu - di-o, Zu - di-o.
2. Step back Sal - ly, Sal - ly, Sal - ly.
3. Go - in' down the al - ley, _ al - ley, _ al - ley, _

Here we go Zu - di-o,
Step ____ back Sal - ly,   } all night long. ____
Go - in' down the al - ley,

DANCE the "Zudio" movement as you sing the song.

MUSICAL SIGNS

Remember the music sign called *repeat*? When two phrases are exactly the same, you don't have to write them twice. You can write the phrase once, then add a repeat sign to each end (||: :||). The refrain from "Killy Kranky" can be written using a repeat sign and a first and second ending.

Refrain
Faster

1.

Broke my arm, broke my arm, swing-in' pret-ty Nan-cy,
Broke my leg, broke my leg,

2.

dan-cin' kil-ly krank-y.

The repeat sign in the **first ending** tells you to go back to the beginning. Then, skip over the first ending to the measures in the **second ending.**

SING the refrain, touching the measures in order as you sing them.

DANCING "KILLY KRANKY"

Many people in the southern Appalachian Mountains, where "Killy Kranky" comes from, are skilled at crafts. They weave baskets, patterns in cloth, even dances!

This picture shows a section of a weaving dance.

"Señor Don Juan de Pancho" comes from the southwestern part of the United States. Many people there speak both Spanish and English.

LISTEN to "Señor Don Juan de Pancho" to find a section in Spanish and a section in English.

Señor DON JUAN de Pancho

New Mexico
Folk Song
English Version
by MMH

Verse

F   C7

Spanish: Se - ñor Don Juan de   Pan-cho, Se - ñor Don Juan de   Dios, ___
Pronunciation: se   nyor don xwan de   pan cho se   nyor don xwan de   ðyos
English: Se - ñor Don Juan de   Pan-cho, Se - ñor Don Juan de   Dios, ___

C7   F

Ma - ña - na se   va pa'l ran-cho; quién sa - be si vol - ve - rá.
ma nya na se ßa   pal ɾan cho kyen sa ße si ßol ße ɾa
To - mor-row he's gone to the ran-cho; and who knows if he'll come back.

B Refrain

Shoo fly, don't both-er me, Shoo fly, don't both-er me,

Shoo fly, don't both-er me, I be-long to Com-pa-ny D.

SING this new melody with words, following the first and second endings.

Shoo, fly! Go a - way. way.
do re re re mi do

LISTEN to "Señor Don Juan de Pancho" and sing this new melody along with the refrain.

A MESSAGE OF GOOD NEWS!

Send a message of good news through art, music, and dance.

Swing Low, Sweet Chariot, 1939, William H. Johnson, THE NATIONAL MUSEUM OF AMERICAN ART, SMITHSONIAN INSTITUTION, Washington, D.C.

SWING LOW, SWEET CHARIOT

In this painting, artist William H. Johnson used long, flowing figures that seem to blend into one another. His choice of warm, rich colors helps to send a comforting message.

SING "Good News" to send a comforting message.

African American Spiritual

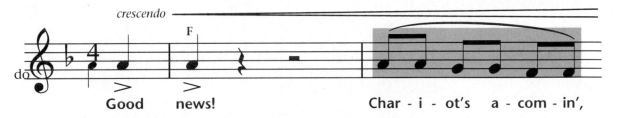

Good news! Char - i - ot's a - com - in',

Good news! Char-i-ot's a-com-in', Good news!

Char-i-ot's a-com-in', and I don't want it to leave me be - hind.

COMPARE "Good News" on page 220 with "Good News" on this page. How are the notes different?

The letter name for the note in the first space is F.

PLAY the tinted notes on bells. Then sing the song, playing A, G, and F on the tinted notes.

A G F

PLAY the melody at the bottom of page 239 on these bells.

Some people in New Mexico perform a dance with "Señor Don Juan de Pancho."

Learn the dance by walking this rhythm through shared space.

Right, left, right, left, right, left.

You've just learned the **ranchero step**!

DANCE the ranchero step, moving counterclockwise during the A section.

WALK four steps toward the middle of the circle and clap on the last step during the B section.

WALK four steps out and clap on the last step. Circle in place for four beats, then stamp, stamp, clap, clap.

Sing Your Message

SING "I Got a Letter," pretending to be happy, sad, mad, or excited about the news in your letter.

I GOT A LETTER

South Carolina
Singing Game

I got a let-ter this morn-ing, Oh, yes.

Oh, yes.

READ the last pitch syllable and name the tonal center.

How are the two phrases alike? How are they different?

CREATE your own phrases using these four pitches.

E
la

G
do

A
re

B
mi

PLAY the rhythm of "I Got a Letter" on any of these bells. Did you end on the tonal center?

You just made your own melody!

Scat singing is made up of nonsense syllables that don't mean anything. Scat was created when jazz singers listened to jazz instruments and used their voices to imitate the sounds they heard.

Spotlight on

ELLA FITZGERALD

Ella Fitzgerald is an American jazz singer known for her scat singing. She started singing as a teenager to earn extra money for her family. When she was eighteen, she wrote and sang her first hit song, "A-Tisket, A-Tasket."

Doodle,

Wah-wah,

It Don't Mean a Thing if It Ain't Got that Swing

LISTENING

by Duke Ellington and Irving Mills

LISTEN to Ella Fitzgerald scat sing in this piece. What scat syllables does she sing?

You can learn to scat sing, too! Listen to "Old Man Moses" to hear scat singing with a song you know.

Choose one of the following scat patterns and sing it in place of the words *Do the hokey pokey and get out of town.*

Imitate the clarinet by singing:

doodle, doodle, doodle, det, det, det!

Imitate the trombone:

wah-wah, wah-wah, wah-wah, woo, woo, wah!

Imitate the trumpet by pinching your nose and singing:

Daba, daba, daba, daba, dat, dat, dot!

CREATE your own scat melodies.

DANCE YOUR MESSAGE

The song "Señor Don Juan de Pancho" comes from New Mexico, where the ranchero step is popular.

PERFORM the ranchero step as you listen to "Señor Don Juan de Pancho."

Form a double circle with a group in your class.

CHOOSE one of the three body-facings pictured for your group.

Front-to-front: partners facing each other

CREATE a dance using the ranchero step. Start your dance in your chosen body-facing. End your dance in a different body-facing.

Side-to-side: partners shoulder-to-shoulder

Back-to-back: partners facing away from each other

In the Appalachian Mountains, the clogging step is popular. The clogging step was originally brought to North America from the British Isles.

PAT this clogging rhythm.

Right, left, right,   left, right, left.

Now step the rhythm.

SING "Killy Kranky" as you perform the clogging step during the verse.

Music

Can you dance?
I love to dance!
Music is my happy chance.
Music playing
In the street
Gets into
My hands and feet

Can you sing?
I love to sing!
Music, like a bird in Spring,
With a gold
And silver note
Gets into
My heart and throat.

Can you play?
I'd love to play!
Practice music everyday—
Then you'll give
The world a chance
To dance and sing,
To sing and dance.

—*Eleanor Farjeon*

These dancers belong to
the Billy Bob Cloggers of
North Carolina.

SONGS MAKING THE HEADLINES

What songs do these headlines suggest?

EXTRA!

SALLY STEPS BACK

MAIL COMES BEFORE NOON

JUAN FLEES INSECTS

CHARIOT REPLACES POST OFFICE TRUCK

DANCING DOCTOR HEALS SENIOR CITIZEN

Say some of these headlines in staccato, marcato, or legato style. Then sing some of the songs using these expressive markings. Which style do you like better? Why?

CHECK IT OUT

1. How is this music sung?

   a. staccato　　**b.** legato　　**c.** marcato

2. How is this music sung?

   a. staccato　　**b.** legato　　**c.** marcato

3. How does this music end?

   a. on the tonal center　　**b.** away from the tonal center

4. How does this music end?

   a. on the tonal center　　**b.** away from the tonal center

5. Which melody do you hear? Is the tonal center of
   that melody *do* or *la,*?

a.

b.

c.

d.

CREATE

Express Yourself

Create a piece of music with first and second endings. Draw these lines on a piece of paper.

Choose some of these rhythms.

Play your piece on instruments. Then perform it using some of the following expressive markings.

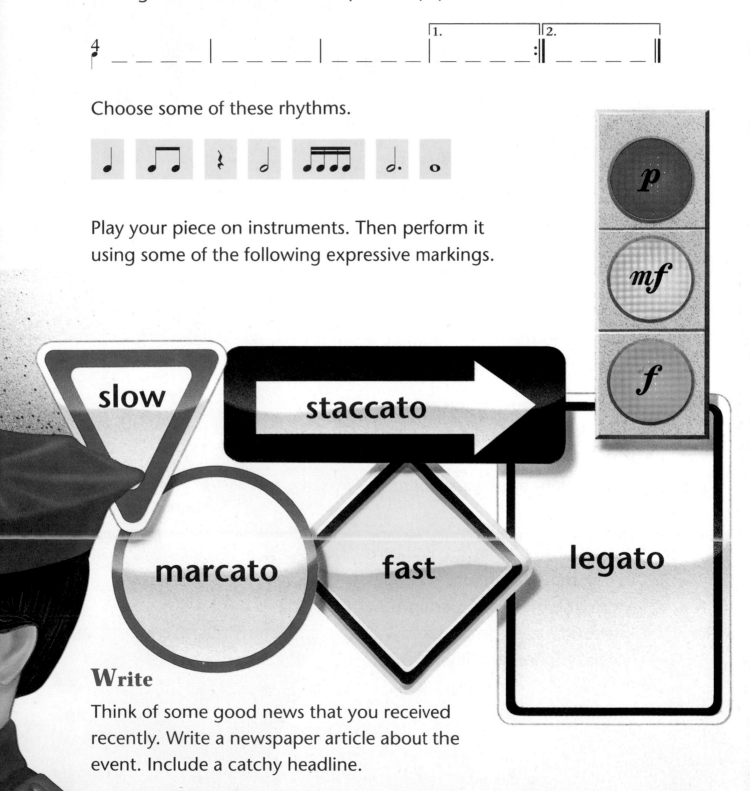

Write

Think of some good news that you received recently. Write a newspaper article about the event. Include a catchy headline.

The Recording studio

Can you imagine a world without music? Watching your favorite television program or listening to the radio would be a very different experience.

Much of the music you enjoy on radio and television is produced in a recording studio. This is a place where musicians record their work.

A studio usually has many rooms. In one room, the performance room, the musicians perform. In another, the control room, specially trained engineers work to make the recording.

THE PERFORMANCE ROOM

The performance room is soundproof. This keeps the
room very quiet while the music is being played.
Microphones pick up the sound of the voices or
instruments. These sounds are recorded on special
equipment located in the control room. When the
performers wear headphones, they can hear the
music that is being recorded. They can also hear what
the people in the control room are saying to them.

THE CONTROL ROOM

The control room has many pieces of equipment. The most important piece is the tape recorder. The size of the tape on this machine is bigger than that on a home tape recorder. It is wider and comes on very large reels.

The different sounds of the recording are put together on a large control, or mixing, board.

The electronic speakers allow the people in the control room to hear what is being recorded. Other equipment helps to make the final recording sound wonderful.

All the rooms have glass walls or large windows. In this way, the performers can see one another. With their headphones, they can also hear one another.

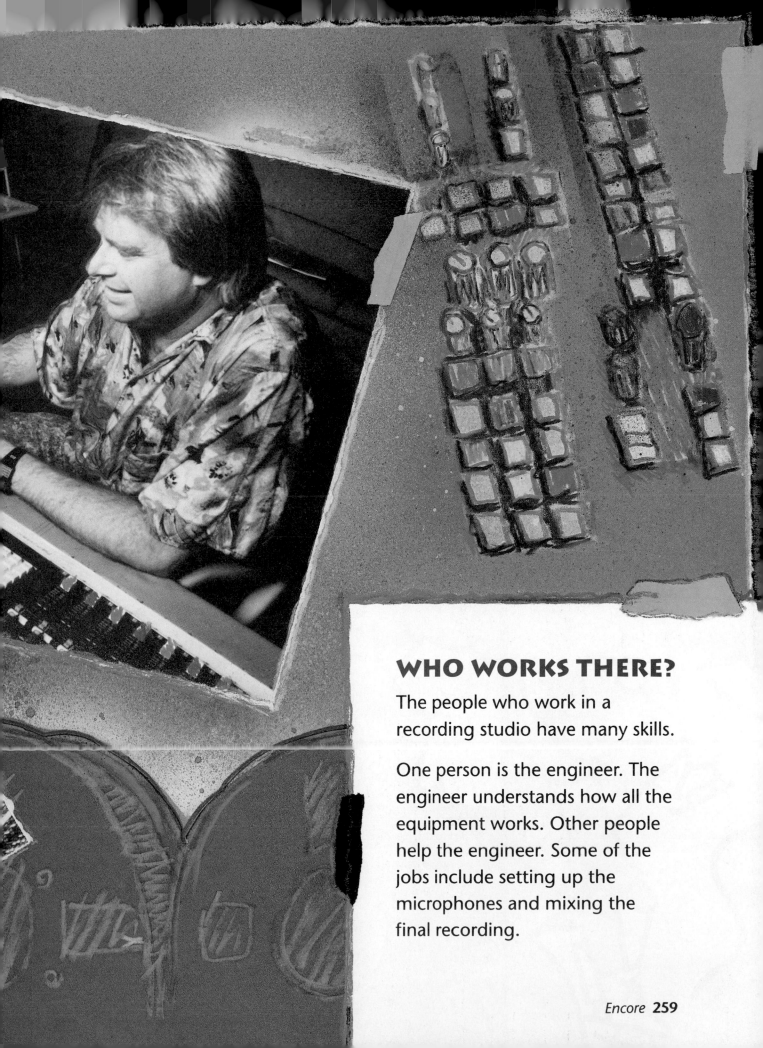

WHO WORKS THERE?

The people who work in a recording studio have many skills.

One person is the engineer. The engineer understands how all the equipment works. Other people help the engineer. Some of the jobs include setting up the microphones and mixing the final recording.

CALENDAR

January shivers,
February shines,
March blows off the winter ice,
April makes the mornings nice,
May is hopscotch lines.

June is deep blue swimming,
Picnics are July,
August is my birthday,
September whistles by.

October is for roller skates,
November is the fireplace,
December is the best because
    of sleds
        and snow
           and Santa Claus.

—*Myra Cohn Livingston*

FROM SEA TO SHINING SEA

Katharine Lee Bates wrote the words to "America, the Beautiful" while visiting Colorado.

Music by
Samuel Ward
Words by
Katharine Lee Bates

America, the Beautiful

O beau-ti-ful for spa-cious skies, For am-ber waves of grain.

For pur-ple moun-tain maj-es-ties, A-bove the fruit-ed plain.

A-mer-i-ca! A-mer-i-ca! God shed His grace on thee,

And crown thy good with broth-er-hood, From sea to shin-ing sea.

You're a Grand Old Flag

Words and Music
by George M. Cohan

You're a grand old flag, you're a high-fly-ing flag;

And for-ev-er in peace may you wave; _____

You're the em-blem of the land I love,

The home of the free and the brave. _____

Ev'-ry heart beats true un-der red, white, and blue,

Where there's nev-er a boast or brag; _____

But should auld ac-quaint-ance be for-got,

Keep your eye on the grand old flag. _____

Woody Guthrie was a composer and folk singer. His songs often describe the beauty of places he visited.

This Land Is Your Land

Words and Music by Woody Guthrie

Refrain

This land is your land, _____ This land is my land, _____ from Cal - i - for - nia _____ to the New York is - land, _____

From the red-wood for - est _____ to the Gulf Stream wa - ters; _____

This land was made for you and me. _____

Verse

1. As I was walk-ing _____ that rib-bon of high-way, _____
2. I've roamed and ram-bled _____ and I fol-lowed my foot-steps _____
3. When the sun comes shin-ing _____ and I was stroll-ing _____

I saw a-bove me _____ that end-less sky-way. _____
to the spar-kling sands of _____ her dia-mond des-erts, _____
and the wheat fields wav-ing _____ and the dust clouds roll-ing, _____

I saw be-low me _____ that gold-en val-ley, _____
And all a-round me _____ a voice was sound-ing, _____
As the fog was lift-ing _____ a voice was chant-ing, _____

Go back to the beginning and sing to the end
(Da Capo al Fine)

This land was made for you and me. _____
"This land was made for you and me." _____
"This land was made for you and me." _____

America

Music by Henry Carey
Words by Samuel F. Smith

My coun-try 'tis of thee, Sweet land of

lib-er-ty, Of thee I sing.

Land where my fa-thers died, Land of the Pil-grim's pride,

From ev'-ry _____ moun-tain-side, Let _____ free-dom ring.

TRICK OR TREAT

They're Out of Sight

Words and Music by
Betty Ann Hunt,
Linda Morgan,
and Brenda Russell

What do the ghosts and gob-lins say on Hal-low-een night?

Boo _____ They give us a fright!

What do the ghosts and gob-lins do on Hal-low-een night? ___

They bump and jump and thump-i-ty thump. They're out of sight! Boo!

List as many Halloween symbols as you can. Then see if you can find them in the poem.

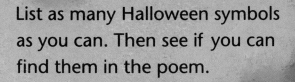

This Is Halloween

Goblins on the doorstep,
Phantoms in the air,
Owls on witches' gateposts
Giving stare for stare,
Cats on flying broomsticks,
Bats against the moon,
Stirrings round of fate-cakes
With a solemn spoon,
Whirling apple parings,
Figures draped in sheets
Dodging, disappearing,
Up and down the streets,
Jack-o'-lanterns grinning,
Shadows on a screen,
Shrieks and starts and laughter—
This is Halloween!

— *Dorothy Brown Thompson*

Many Halloween customs come from other countries. The Irish were the first to make jack-o'-lanterns from large potatoes and turnips. In the United States, pumpkins became popular. Pumpkins make bigger, scarier faces!

Halloween Night

Words and Music
by Doris Parker

Refrain

f Dm

Bet - ter watch out, it's Hal - low - een night.

Dm   A7   Dm

Look at all the spook - y sights. ___

Dm

Bet - ter watch out it's Hal - low - een night.

Dm   A7   Dm

End (Fine)

Look at all the spook - y sights. ___

Name sound effects you could use to create a spooky feeling. Share your sound effects with the class as you sing the song.

Verse

1. Skel - e - tons, let's have some fun.
2. Witch - es, too, what can you do?
3. Gob-lins and ghosts, how can you fly?

When I count to eight, you must be done. ___
When I count to eight, you must be through. _
When I count to eight, come down from the sky. ___

Go back to the beginning and sing to the end
(Da Capo al Fine)

p

One two three four five six seven eight.

HARVEST TIME

The tradition of having a celebration at harvest time is thousands of years old. In the United States, Thanksgiving is an important harvest celebration. People everywhere celebrate the earth's gifts.

Gather 'Round

Words and Music
by Margaret C. duGard

Raise your voice with __ joy - ous __ ring - ing, Gath - er 'round hear __ chil - dren sing - ing. Ding, dong, ding, ring - a - ling, Ding, dong, ding, ring - a - ling. Give thanks and sing, Give

thanks and sing. Young folks gath-er 'round.

Old folks gath-er 'round. Gath-er 'round and join us sing-ing,

Ding, dong, ding, ring-a-ling, Ding, dong, ding, ring-a-ling. Give

thanks and sing, Give thanks and sing.

SUKKOT AND SHAVUOT

Sukkot is a Jewish celebration of the fall harvest. A long time ago, farmers built huts in their fields to stay in during harvest. Today, families build small shelters to celebrate that tradition.

Shavuot, another Jewish festival, celebrates the end of the grain harvest and the beginning of the fruit harvest. Shavuot is a time of sharing with friends and family.

Hag Asif describes the time of Sukkot.

HAG ASIF
Harvest Time

Words and Music
by S. Levy Tannai
English Version by L. Koulish

Refrain

Hebrew: חַג אָ-סִיף, חַג אָ-סִיף כֵּן יִרְ-בֶּה ו-כֵן יֹו-סִיף.

Pronunciation: xag a sif   xag a sif   ken yir be və   xen yo sif

English: **Har-vest time,   har-vest time.   Gath-er in the   gold-en wheat.**

Verse

בַּ-שָׂ-דֶה חָ-לַף קָ-צִיר

ba sa dε xa laf ka tsir

1. In the mead - ow as we ___ walk,
2. Draw the wa - ter from the ___ well,
3. Thanks for days that come and ___ go, The

וּ-בַ-כֶּ-רֶם תַּם בָּ-צִיר

u va kε rεm tam ba tsir

Wheat is rip-en - ing on the ___ stalk.
See the fruits of har - vest ___ swell.
warmth of the sun and the fall - ing ___ snow.

וְ-עַ-תָּה עִם בֹּא הַ-סְתָו

və a ta im bo has tav

Wield the scythe and cut the grain,
Build the suk - kot tall and strong.
Thanks for our food and the crops that grow, The

272 HARVEST TIME

xag a sif na xog bə shir.

Au - tumn	sea - son's	here	a -	gain.
Join our	hands in	dance	and ___	song.
love we	share and the	friends	we ___	know.

Shavuot is the festival that celebrates the first fruits of spring. It is a good occasion to sing and dance.

HAG SHAVUOT
Festival of First Fruits

Traditional Israeli
Holiday Song
English Version by MMH

Hebrew: חַג שָׁ - בוּ - עוֹת חַג שָׁ - בוּ - עוֹת חַג שָׁ - בוּ - עוֹת הַ -
Pronunciation: xag sha vu ot xag sha vu ot xag sha vu ot hi
English: **Hag Sha-vu - ot,** hag sha-vu - ot, hag sha-vu - ot the ___

זֶה נֶה בָּא. עַל רָא - שֵׁי - נוּ זֵר פְּרָ - חִים
nё zε ba al ɾɔ she nu zeɾ pɾɑ xim

| fruit is here. | We shall dress our | hair with gar - lands |

בְּ - יָ - דֵי - נוּ בִּ - כּוּ - רִים בִּ - כּוּ - רִים.
bə ya de nu bi ku ɾim bi ku ɾim

| car - ry first fruits ___ | in our hands. | in our hands. |

WINTER

FEST

Winter festivals in Japan honor the beauty of the ice and snow. People in northern Japan hold a Snow Hut Festival. Families build special snow huts for the celebration.

YUKI
SNOW

Japanese School Song
English Version by MMH

F

Japanese: ゆ － き や こん こん あ ら れ や こん こん
Pronunciation: yu ki ya kon kon a ɾa ɾe ya kon kon
English: **Snow is fall-ing,** *kon,* *kon.* **Hail is fall-ing,** *kon,* *kon.*

F   C7

ふっ て は ふっ て は ずん ずん つ も る
fut te wa fut te wa zuṇ zuṇ tsu mo ɾu
Snow fall-ing, snow drift-ing, down __down __ hail and snow.

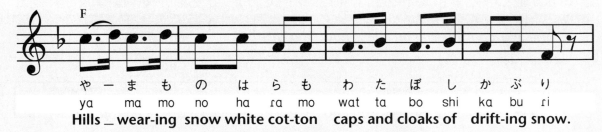

F

や － ま も の は ら も わ た ぼ し か ぶ り
ya ma mo no ha ɾa mo wat ta bo shi ka bu ɾi
Hills _ wear-ing snow white cot-ton caps and cloaks of drift-ing snow.

B♭   F   C7   F

か れ き の こ ら ず は な が さ く
ka ɾe ki no ko ɾa zu ha na ga sa ku
There on the cold, bare branch-es snow flow'rs are in bloom.

274

St. Stephen's Day, or Boxing Day, is the day after Christmas. In England long ago, boys would carry a wren from door to door to bring each house good luck.

The Wren Song

Irish Folk Song

1. The wren, the wren, the king of all birds,
2. We fol-lowed the wren three miles ___ or more,
3. Rol - ley, Rol - ley, where's ___ your nest?
4. As I went out to hunt ___ and all,
5. I have a lit-tle box un - der me arm,

Saint Ste - phen's Day was caught in the firs;
Three miles or more, three miles ___ or more,
It's in the bush that I _____ love best,
I met a wren up - on ___ the wall,
A tup-pence or pen-ny - 'll do it no harm,

Al - though he was lit - tle, his hon - or was great,
Through hedg - es and ditch - es and heaps ___ of snow,
It's in ___ the bush, ___ the hol - ly tree,
Up with me wat - tle and gave him a fall,
For we are the boys ___ that came ___ your way

Jump up, me lads, and give us a treat!
At six o' - clock in the morn - ing.
Where all the boys do fol - low me.
And brought him here to show ___ you all.
To bring in the wren on St. Ste - phen's Day!

EIGHT DAYS OF LIGHT

The story of Hanukkah tells how a little oil kept the holy lamps in Jerusalem burning for eight days. The holiday is celebrated by lighting candles. Eight candles are placed in a candleholder called a *menorah*. Each night, a ninth candle is used to light one more candle. On the last night of Hanukkah, all of the lights burn brightly together.

O, Hanukkah

Jewish Folk Song
English Version by MMH

Yiddish: אוי, אַ נֶער שֵׁיי אַ טֶאב אַ יוֹן אַ ,כָּה-נוּ-חֶ אוֹי ,כָּה-נוּ-חֶ
Pronunciation: o xɑn u kɑ o xɑn u kɑ ɑ yɔn tɛf ɑ she nər ɑ
English: O Ha-nuk-kah, O Ha-nuk-kah, a beau-ti-ful sea-son, a

.נֶער זוֹי-אַ נָאך טֶא נִי ,כֶער-לֶע-פֿרֵיי-אַ ,קֶער-טִי-לוֹס
lus tig ər a frɛ lix ər ni to nɔx a zɛɪ nər
joy-ous hap-py fes-ti-val un-like an-y oth-er.

מִיר, לֶן-שׁפִּי דֶלֶעך-דרֵיי אִין נָאכֿט לֶע-אַ
a lə naxt in dred lax shpi lən mir
Spin-ning, turn-ing drey-dls and good things to eat;

Joy of Christmas

People in many parts of the world celebrate Christmas on December 25. This holiday honors the birth of Jesus. In the United States, people of different backgrounds share holiday songs and customs.

Children, Go Where I Send Thee

African American Carol

(Cumulative: For each new verse, add lines above.)

Chil-dren, go where I send thee; How shall I send thee? I will send thee { one by one. __ / two by two. __ / three by three. __ / four by four. __ / five by five. __ } Well,

1. One was the lit - tle bit - ty ba - by, ___
2. Two was the Paul __ and __ Si - las, ___
3. Three was the three __ men __ rid - ing, ___
4. Four was the four __ come a - knock - ing at the door,
5. Five was the Gos - pel __ preach - ers, ___

Wrapped in swad-dling cloth-ing, __ Ly-ing in the man-ger. __

Born, born, __ oh, __ Born in Beth-le-hem. __

6. Six was the six who couldn't get fixed, . . .

7. Seven was the seven who went to heaven, . . .

8. Eight was the eight who stood by the gate, . . .

9. Nine was the nine who saw the sign, . . .

10. Ten was the Ten Commandments, . . .

What do you say when you are excited or happy? Some people shout "Hallelu!" What other words do you know that express the same feeling?

Wasn't That a MIGHTY Day?

African American Folk Song

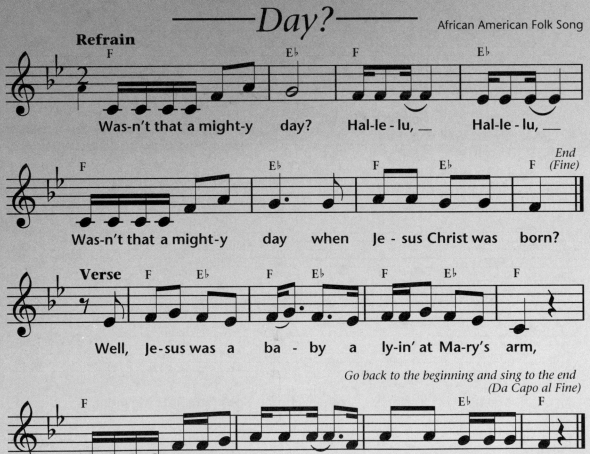

Refrain

Was-n't that a might-y day? Hal-le-lu, ___ Hal-le-lu, ___

Was-n't that a might-y day when Je - sus Christ was born?

Verse

Well, Je-sus was a ba - by a ly-in' at Ma-ry's arm,

Go back to the beginning and sing to the end
(Da Capo al Fine)

Ly-in' in the sta-ble at Beth-le-hem, the beasts they keep-a him warm.

Members of The Boys Choir of Harlem

The story of Christmas is very old. Any story that is told over and over sounds a little different each time. That is why stories and songs about the birth of Jesus are alike in some ways and different in other ways.

LISTENING

Great Day in December by C. Jeter

In this music, one man sings the words that tell the Christmas story. He has a very high voice. Four other men sing with him in the background. How is the story in this song the same or different from others you have heard?

The Christmas story tells of three kings who brought gifts. This poem is about one of those men. His name was Balthazar. Why does the poet think Balthazar was special?

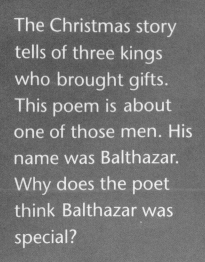

Carol
of the
BROWN KING

Of the three Wise Men
Who came to the King,
One was a brown man,
So they sing.

Of the three Wise Men
Who followed the Star,
One was a brown king
From afar.

They brought fine gifts
Of spices and gold
In jeweled boxes
Of beauty untold.

Unto His humble
Manger they came
And bowed their heads
In Jesus' name.

Three Wise Men,
One dark like me—
Part of His
Nativity.

—Langston Hughes

Members of African American churches often answer
the preacher. The people say "Hallelu!" or "That's
right!" or "Amen!"

AMEN

African American Spiritual
Additional Words by MMH

A - men, A - men,

A - men, A - men, A - men, men. See the

(1.) ba - by,   Ly - ing in the   man-ger,
(2.) Moth - er,   Sing - in' to the   ba - by,   } One Christ-mas morn-ing,
(3.) Shep-herds,   Come to see the   ba - by,

All

A - men, A - men, A - men.
A - men, A - men, A - men.
A - men, A - men, A - men. Sing it soft-er now,

first time only

A - men,   A - men,

last time only

A - men, A - men, A - men, Sing it strong-er now, _ men.

Group may continue with "Amen" throughout solo part.   Celebrations *Christmas* **283**

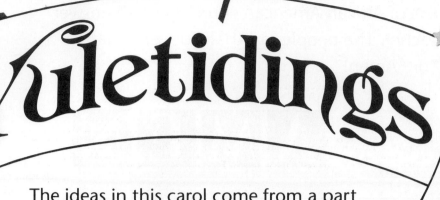

Yuletidings

The ideas in this carol come from a part
of the Bible called the Book of Psalms.
When you sing the song, let your
glad feelings show!

Joy to the
WORLD

Music by Lowell Mason
English Poem by Isaac Watts

do

D   G   A7   D

Joy   to   the   world!   the   Lord   is   come.

Let earth re - ceive her King.

Let ev' - ry __ heart __ pre - pare __ Him __ room. __

And heav'n and na-ture _ sing, And _ heav'n and na-ture _ sing,

And _ heav'n, _ and heav'n __ and na - ture sing.

This carol was first sung many years ago in France.
Which words in the song make the sound of a flute?
Which ones make the sound of a drum?

Pat-a-Pan

Burgundian
French Carol
English Version
by Merrill Staton

1.   Wil - lie take your lit - tle drum, Rob-in bring your flute and come.
2.   When the lit - tle child was born long a - go that Christ-mas morn,
3.   Now we cel - e-brate this day on our in - stru-ments we play.

Play   a   joy - ous tune to - day.
Shep-herds came from fields a - far, Tu-re-lu-re - lu, pat-a-pat-a - pan,
Let our voi - ces loud-ly ring,

Play   a   joy - ous tune to - day on this joy - ous hol - i - day.
Shep-herds came from fields a - far guid-ed by the shin-ing star.
Let our voi - ces loud-ly ring, as our song and gifts we bring.

"Deck the Hall" describes the joyful custom of decorating for Christmas. The song comes from Wales, where singing contests are held the week before Christmas.

Deck the Hall

Welsh Carol

Gaily

1. Deck the hall with boughs of hol-ly,
2. See the blaz-ing yule be-fore us,
3. Fast a-way the old year pass-es,
} Fa la la la la, la la la la,

'Tis the sea-son to be jol-ly,
Strike the harp and join the cho-rus,
Hail the new, ye lads and lass-es,
} Fa la la la la, la la la la,

Don we now our gay ap-par-el,
Fol-low me in mer-ry mea-sure,
Sing we joy-ous all to-geth-er,
} Fa la la la la la la, la la la,

Troll the an-cient yule-tide car-ol,
While I tell of yule-tide trea-sure,
Heed-less of the wind and weath-er,
} Fa la la la la, la la la la.

The farmer in this song was preparing his piglets for the holiday. Read Verses 3 and 4 to find out what happened!

The PIGLETS' Christmas

American Folk Song
Words by Mary Goetze
and Nancy Cooper
Arranged by Mary Goetze

Spirited
Verse *mf*

1. On the day be - fore Christ - mas the
2. He had fed them with bar - ley and
3. O he dashed them with bur - net and
4. As he heat - ed the ov - en it
5. O the pigs sang a car - ol, the

farm - er did boast That his pig - lets were
fed them with corn So they'd be nice and
ba - sil and bay. They were but - tered and
came ver - y clear, That he nev - er could
farm - er sang too, With the feast - ing for -

Refrain

Cm7   F   Cm7

best   for   the   hol - i - day   roast.
fat   for   the   feast   Christ - mas   morn.
bread - ed   to   bake   for   a   day. } Tra   la
eat   them   for   they   were   too   dear.
got - ten   a - midst   the   to - do.

F   Cm7   F   Cm7

la   la   la   la   la   la   la   la   la   Tra   la

F   Cm7   F   Cm7   F

la   la   la   la   la   la   la   la   la.

From HOUSE to HOUSE

In England many years ago, friends greeted each other at holiday time with "Was haile!" These words meant "Be healthy!" When carolers sang from house to house, their neighbors gave them a hot drink to warm themselves.

Here We Come A-Wassailing

English Carol

Verse

1. Here we come a - was-sail - ing   a - mong the leaves so green, ____
2. are not dai - ly beg - gars that beg from door to door.   We
3. bless the mas-ter   of this house, like-wise the mis-tress too,   And

Here we come   a - wan-d'ring so   fair ____ to be   seen;
are your neigh-bor's chil - dren whom you have seen be - fore.
all the lit - tle   chil - dren that   round the ta - ble   go.

Refrain

Love and joy come to you, And to you your was-sail too,

And God bless you and send you a hap - py New Year,

1.,2.

3.

And God send you a hap - py New Year.

2. We Year.
3. God

This poem from *The Wind in the Willows* is about a chorus of mice who visit their neighbors, the Rat and the Mole.

from CAROL

Villagers all, this frosty tide,
Let your doors swing open wide.
Though wind may follow, and snow beside,
Yet draw us in by your fire to bide;
Joy shall be yours in the morning!

Here we stand in the cold and the sleet,
Blowing fingers and stamping feet,
Come from far away to greet —
You by the fire and we in the street —
Bidding you joy in the morning!

— Kenneth Grahame

Everybody Says Freedom

Martin Luther King, Jr., Day celebrates the birthday of Dr. King. He fought for equality and justice for African Americans and people everywhere.

WOKE UP THIS MORNING

Freedom Song

Woke up this morn-ing with my mind _____ stayed on free - dom. ___

Woke up this morn-ing with my heart _____ stayed on free - dom. ___

Woke up this morn-ing with my soul _____ stayed on free - dom. __

Hal-le - lu, hal-le-lu, hal-le - lu, hal-le-lu, hal-le - lu - jah.

End
(Fine)

I'm gon-na walk, talk, __ sing, shout, _ hal - le - lu __ I got my

mind on free-dom. Walk, talk __ sing, shout, _ clap my hands and keep my

Go back to the beginning and sing to the end
(Da Capo al Fine)

mind on free-dom. Walk, talk, _ sing, shout, _ clap my hands. _

I'm on My Way to Freedom Land

LISTENING

Adaptation of a traditional song

During the 1960s, songs about equality for African Americans became popular. Songs like this one made everyone aware of Dr. King's dream.

DESCRIBE what you think a place called Freedom Land would be like.

Be My Valentine

A favorite Valentine's Day custom is sending cards or flowers. Some messages aren't signed so that the name of the sender is a secret. Do you think this song is for a friend?

Never Gonna Be Your Valentine

Words and Music by Linda Worsley

1. I don't wan - na be your val - en - tine,
2. I'm not gon - na be your val - en - tine,
3. I might wan - na be your val - en - tine,

I don't wan - na be your val - en - tine,
I'm not gon - na be your val - en - tine,
I might wan - na be your val - en - tine,

Don't wan - na be your val - en - tine to - day!
You're not the kind of val - en - tine I like!
Don't tell a soul, 'cause you know ver - y well

Irish Eyes Are Smiling

We celebrate St. Patrick's Day with parades, shamrocks, and by wearing green. Green is a reminder of the Irish land.

St. Patrick's Day

LISTENING

by Leo Rowsome

Leo Rowsome was a famous Irish piper. He learned to make and play the pipes from his father and grandfather. Bagpipes are filled with air. The air is pushed through a pipe to make its sound. The Irish pipes are played without blowing the air–instead the player pumps the air into the bag with his or her arm.

This Irish folk song is about a man who
works hard and is proud of it.

The Wee Falorie Man

Irish Folk Song
Collected by
David Hammond

1. I am the wee Fa - lo - rie man,
2. I am a good old work - in' man,

A rat - tlin', rov - in' I - rish - man,
Each day I car - ry my wee tin can, A

I can do all that ev - er you can, For
large pen - ny bap and a clipe ____ of ham,

I am the wee Fa - lo - rie man.
I am a good old work - in' man.

Cherry Blossom Time

Cherry trees and their delicate blossoms are a special part of Japanese spring celebrations. Every year families go on a picnic and view the cherry blossoms.

Japanese Americans celebrate the cherry blooms as well as their Japanese culture. The Cherry Blossom Festival in San Francisco includes music, dance, art, and food. In Washington, D.C., people enjoy the cherry trees that were a gift from the mayor of Tokyo, Japan, in 1912.

SAKURA
CHERRY BLOSSOMS

Japanese Folk Song
English Version by MMH

Japanese: さくら さくら やよいの そらは
Pronunciation: sa ku ɾa sa ku ɾa ya yo i no so ɾa wa
English: **Cher-ry tree, Cher-ry tree! Cher-ry blos-soms ev'-ry - where.**

みわたす かぎり かすみか くもか
mi wa ta su ka gi ɾi ka su mi ka ku mo ka
Far as an-y eye can _ see. Mist and beau-ty fill the _ air,

に　お　い　ぞ　い　ず　る　い　ざ　や　い　ざ　や
ni　o　i　zo　i　zu　ru　i　za　ya　i　za　ya
Love-ly blos-soms scent the _breeze. Come with me, come with me,

み　に　ゆ　か　ん
mi　ni　yu　ka　n
Let ____ us go ____ and see.

These short Japanese poems are
called *haiku.* Many haiku show
love and respect for nature.

**Ashes my burnt hut
But wonderful the cherry
Blooming on the hill.**

—*Hokushi*

**In the black branches
beautiful cherry blossoms
pink, white and little.**

—*Mitsu Salmon, Age 10*

Voices of the Earth

The Pygmies live in the rain forest in the Central African Republic. The forest gives them food, clothing, warmth, and a feeling of friendship.

This is a song and dance that celebrates the earth and all growing things. *Ema* means mother. The rest of the words have no special meaning, but are there just to sing.

Ema, Ma

Pygmy Dance Song

Group 1

A Bantu Dialect: **A - i - ba   e, _____   A - i - ba   e - ma, __ ma __**
Pronunciation: ɑ   i   bɑ   ɛ   ɑ   i   bɑ   ɛ   mɑ   mɑ

Group 2   **Group 3**

E -   ma, __ ma __   A - i - ba   e. _____
ɛ   mɑ   mɑ   ɑ   i   bɑ   ɛ

From Morning Night to Real Morning

LISTENING

Voices of the rain forest collected by Steven Feld

Before the sun comes up, the rain forest is alive with the rhythm of insects, tree frogs, and dripping leaves. Listen for these sounds. You will also hear the voices of more than 150 different kinds of birds singing.

DANCE OF THE ANIMALS

I throw myself to the left,
I turn myself to the right,
I am the fish
Who glides in the water, who glides,
Who twists himself, who leaps.
Everything lives, everything dances, everything sings.

The bird flies,
Flies, flies, flies,
Goes, comes back, passes,
Mounts, hovers, and drops down.
I am the bird.
Everything lives, everything dances, everything sings.

The monkey, from bough to bough,
Runs, leaps, and jumps,
With his wife, with his little one,
His mouth full, his tail in the air:
This is the monkey, this is the monkey.
Everything lives, everything dances, everything sings.

—Pygmy Song

"All Living Things" reminds us that all life on Earth is connected.

NAME the living things in this song.

ALL LIVING THINGS

Words and Music by W. Jay Cawley

Verse

1. All liv-ing things _____ need the air to breathe, __
2. All liv-ing things _____ need the warm sun-shine, __
3. All liv-ing things _____ need to have a home, __

Need the sky __ up a-bove, __ the earth be-neath their feet. __
Need the cool __ sum-mer breeze, __ that blows on down the line. __
Need a place _ to rest __ their heads, __ a pur-pose of their own. __

For the fish-es in __ the o-cean and the birds that sing, __
For the ap-ples in __ the or-chards and the flow-ers in __ the spring, __
We must live __ to-geth-er __ so let us dance and sing, __

This world ____ is the home __ of liv-ing things. things.

Interlude

If we clear a-way _ the for - est _____

strip the land, ____ spoil the sea, ____

what will there ___ be left ___ for us to love _

Go back to Verse 3 and sing to the end

_ in this world of liv-ing things?

SUMMER FOLKLIFE

Each August over 30 different groups of people gather in San Antonio, Texas, for the Texas Folklife Festival. A folklife festival, or fair, is a way to honor and celebrate different customs and traditions.

You can celebrate traditions anytime with songs, dances, and games. Summer folklife includes everything from barbershop quartets to polkas.

SAN ANTONIO ★

In the Good Old Summertime

Music by
George Evans
Words by
Ron Shields

In the good old sum - mer - time. _____

In the good old sum-mer-time. _____

304

Strolling through the shady lanes, with your baby mine. You hold her hand and she holds yours. And that's a very good sign. That she's your tootsey wootsey in the good old summertime.

LISTENING

In the Good Old Summertime

Music by George Evans
Words by Ron Shields

Only one person sings the melody in a barbershop quartet. Three other people sing harmony.

LISTEN to a barbershop quartet sing. How is it different from the way you sing this song?

Folk dancing is popular at summer festivals.
Try this dance with a partner.

Cotton-Eyed Joe

American Dance Song

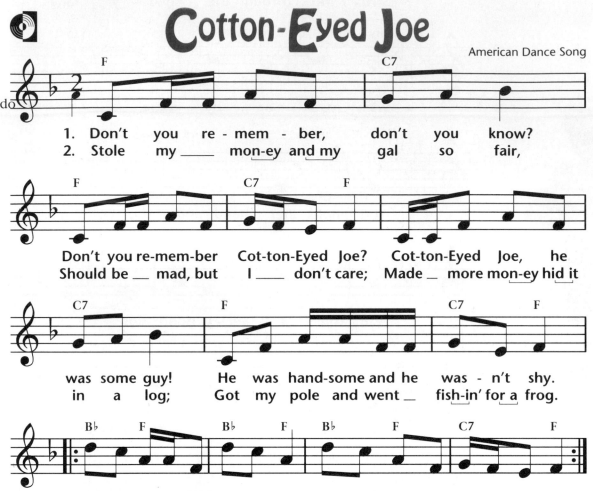

1. Don't you re-mem-ber, don't you know?
2. Stole my _____ mon-ey and my gal so fair,

Don't you re-mem-ber Cot-ton-Eyed Joe? Cot-ton-Eyed Joe, he
Should be __ mad, but I ___ don't care; Made __ more mon-ey hid it

was some guy! He was hand-some and he was-n't shy.
in a log; Got my pole and went __ fish-in' for a frog.

Hold my fid-dle and hold my bow, watch me dance like Cot-ton-Eyed Joe.

Brush　　　　　**Kick**

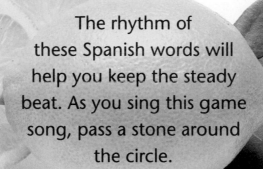

The rhythm of these Spanish words will help you keep the steady beat. As you sing this game song, pass a stone around the circle.

ACITRÓN

Spanish Stone-Passing Game

Spanish: A - ci - trón de un fan - dan-go, zan-go, zan-go, sa-ba - ré.
Pronunciation: a si trɔn de um fan dan go san go san go sa βa ɾe

Sa-ba - ré de far - an - de - la, con su tri-qui, tri-qui tran.
sa βa ɾe ðe faɾ an de la kon su tri ki tri ki tran

307

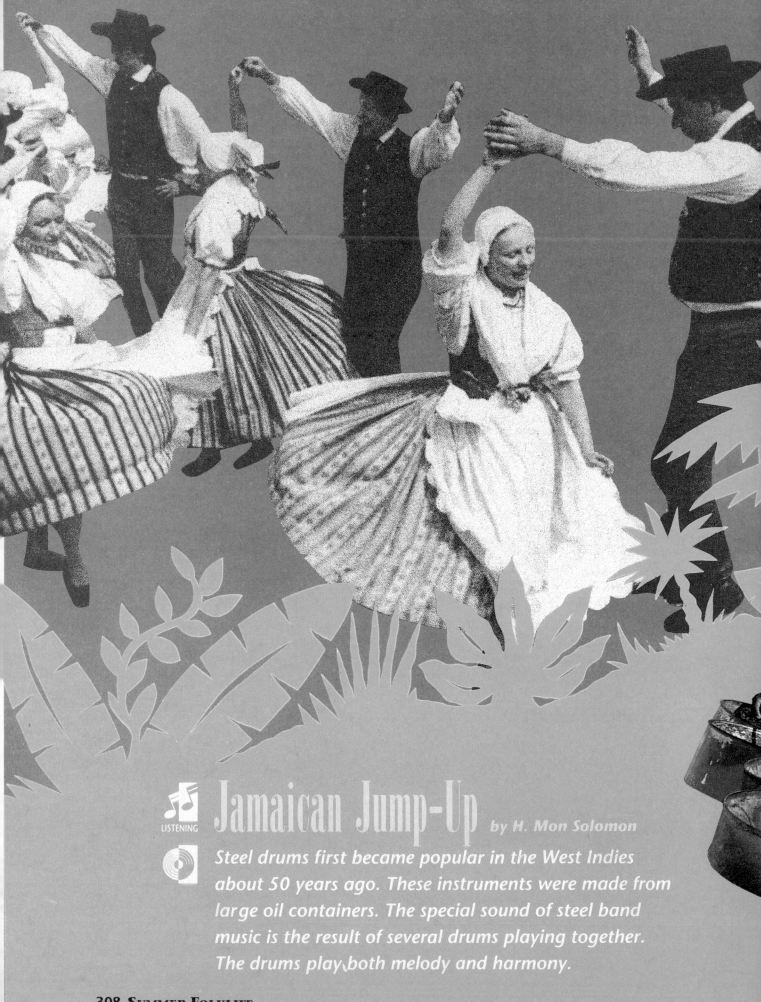

Jamaican Jump-Up

by H. Mon Solomon

Steel drums first became popular in the West Indies about 50 years ago. These instruments were made from large oil containers. The special sound of steel band music is the result of several drums playing together. The drums play both melody and harmony.

Doudlebska Polka

Traditional Czech Polka

The polka is a dance that started among the Czech people almost 200 years ago. It quickly spread throughout Europe. Now people everywhere dance the polka. Doudlebska is a town in Southwest Bohemia. The word doudlebska means "double clap" in English. As you hear this polka performed by the Shenanigans, listen for a place to clap twice.

HOT CROSS BUNS

English Street Cry

Hot cross buns, hot cross buns,

One a pen-ny, two a pen-ny, hot cross buns.

Farfallina Butterfly

Italian Folk Song
English Version by MMH

Italian: Far-fal-li-na tut-ta bian-ca vo-la, vo-la, non si stan-ca.
Pronunciation: far fal li na tut ta byang ka vo la vo la non si stang ka
English: Far-fal-li-na, with your white wings, fly a-way, do not sit still. _

Vo-la li, vo-la la, po-si po-sa so-pra un fiore.
vo la li vo la la po si po sa so praun fyore
Fly-ing here, fly-ing there, on a flow-er rest a while.

GREAT BIG HOUSE

Louisiana Play Party Song

F   C7

1. Great big house in New Or - leans,   For - ty sto - ries high; ___
2. Went down to the old mill stream, To fetch a   pail of wa - ter;
3. Fare thee well, my dar-ling girl,   Fare thee well, my daugh-ter;

F   C7   F

Ev' - ry room that I   been in,   Filled with chick - en pie.
Put one arm   a-round my wife, The   o - ther 'round my daugh-ter.
Fare thee well, my dar - ling girl, with the gold - en slip - pers on her.

Yangtze Boatmen's Chantey

Sea Chantey

River boat-men we, Toil-ing night and day.

Backs bend-ing, Ropes tight-'ning, Sing we loud our lay.

'Simmons

Alabama Singing Game

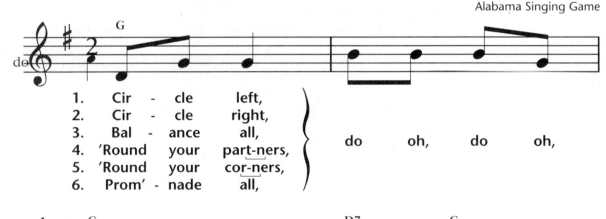

1. Cir - cle left,
2. Cir - cle right,
3. Bal - ance all,
4. 'Round your part-ners,
5. 'Round your cor-ners,
6. Prom' - nade all,

do oh, do oh,

Cir - cle left,
Cir - cle right,
Bal - ance all,
'Round your part-ners,
'Round your cor-ners,
Prom'-nade all,

do oh, do oh,

Cir - cle left,
Cir - cle right,
Bal - ance all,
'Round your part-ners,
'Round your cor-ners,
Prom'-nade all,

do oh, do oh, Shake them 'sim - mons down!

Chichipapa
The Sparrows' Singing School

Japanese Folk Song
English Version by MMH

Japanese:	チ	チ	パッ	パ	チ	パッ	パ
Pronunciation:	chi	chi	pap	pa	chi	pap	pa
English:	**Chi**	**chi**	**pa**	**pa,**	**Chi**	**pa**	**pa!**

す	ず	め	の	がっ	こう	の	せん	せい	は
su	zu	me	no	gak	ko	no	sen	sei	wa
Teach-er		**of**	**the**	**spar-rows'** __			**sing-**	**ing**	**school.**

ム	チ	を	ふ	り	ふ	り	チ	パッ	パ
mu	chi	o	fu	ɾi	fu	ɾi	chi	pap	pa
Waves a		**stick**	**to**	**lead**	**us**	**sing-ing**		**Chi**	**pa** **pa!**

チ	チ	パッ	パ	チ	パッ	パ
chi	chi	pap	pa	chi	pap	pa
Chi	**chi**	**pa**	**pa,**	**Chi**	**pa**	**pa!**

One, Two, Three O'Leary

Children's Game Song

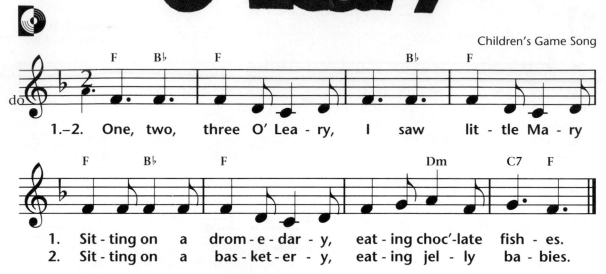

1.–2. One, two, three O' Lea - ry, I saw lit - tle Ma - ry

1. Sit - ting on a drom - e - dar - y, eat - ing choc'-late fish - es.
2. Sit - ting on a bas - ket - er - y, eat - ing jel - ly ba - bies.

SCOTLAND'S BURNING

Traditional Round

Scot-land's burn-ing, Scot-land's burn-ing, Look out! Look out!

Fire! fire! fire! fire! Pour on wa - ter, Pour on wa - ter.

314

Treasure Chests

Words and Music by Minnie O'Leary

Verse

1. Some of us come from a dis-tant land, Some of us from near-
2. Treas - ures come from _ years a-go from coun - tries far a -
3. Hol - i-days, games and _ stor - ies, Lan - gua-ges and ___

by, But all of us car - ry a treas - ure chest With
way, _____ Treas - ures come from our fam - i - lies, Last
songs; _____ Faith _ and cour - age and wis - dom, And

things that gold can't buy; with things that gold can't buy.
year or yes - ter - day; last year or yes - ter - day.
ways to get a - long; and ways to get a - long.

Refrain

And when we share our treas - ure chests we

all grow rich, you see. The rich - es in that treas-ure chest are

what makes you and me; are what makes you and me.

Skip to My Lou

American Play Song

1. Flies in the but - ter - milk, Shoo fly, shoo,
2. Lit-tle red ____ wag - on paint - ed blue;
3. Lost my ____ part - ner, what'll I do?
4. I'll find an - oth - er one, bet-ter than you;
5. Lou, ____ lou, ____ skip to my lou;

Flies in the but - ter - milk, Shoo fly, shoo,
Lit-tle red ____ wag - on paint - ed blue;
Lost my ____ part - ner, what'll I do?
I'll find an - oth - er one, bet-ter than you;
Lou, ____ lou, ____ skip to my lou;

Flies in the but - ter - milk, Shoo fly, shoo,
Lit-tle red ____ wag - on paint - ed blue;
Lost my ____ part - ner, what'll I do?
I'll find an - oth - er one, bet-ter than you;
Lou, ____ lou, ____ skip to my lou;

Skip to my lou, my dar - ling.

Miss Mary Mack

African American Singing Game

1. Miss Ma - ry Mack, Mack, Mack,
2. She asked her moth-er, moth-er, moth-er,
3. They jumped so high, high, high,

All dressed in black, black, black,
For fif - ty cents, cents, cents,
They reached the sky, sky, sky,

With sil - ver but-tons, but-tons, but-tons,
To see the cows, __ cows, __ cows, __
And nev-er came back, __ back, __ back, __

All down her back, back, back.
Jump o-ver the fence, fence, fence.
Till the Fourth of Ju - ly, lie, lie!

The Delta Queen

Words and Music
by Fran Smartt Andicott

A

1. Work - ing on the Del - ta Queen,
2. Old deck shoes and worn blue jeans.
3. Not a show for the sil - ver screen.
4. You'll be glad you made the scene.

tough-est job you've ev - er ___ seen.   This old riv - er's
Make a meal of pork __ and __ beans.   Riv - er boat stands
Boat's new pas-sen-gers turn - in' __ green.   This old riv - er's a
I've been here since I turned __ eight - een.   Want to see a

End (Fine)

brown and green;   Trick - y cur - rents make her mean. __
tall and lean,   Keep her decks all spot - less clean. __
tough ma - rine.   For teach - ing les - sons, she's the dean. __
real ma - chine?   Come and ride the Del - ta Queen! __

B

Swing

1.–3.   Won't you come a-long with me   (ch   ch ___)

318

might-y Mis-sis-sip-pi (ch ch ___) { will give us a ride. ___
{ is a sight to ___ see. ___
{ keeps flow-in' ___ south. ___

Go back to the beginning and sing to the end
(Da Capo al Fine)

(ch ch ___) She's got old St. Lou-is right at her side. _____
(ch ch ___) Rock-in' and rol-lin' past Mem-phis, Ten - nes - see.
(ch ch ___) She's got New Or-leans' ___ foot in her mouth. _____

Go 'Round the Mountain

Illinois Play Party Song

Leader
F

Group
C7   F   C7

1. Go 'round the moun-tain;
2. Swing 'round your part - ner;
3. Back 'round the moun-tain;
4. Girls through the win - dow;
5. Boys through the win - dow;
6. Find you a new love;

} To-di-did-dle-um, To-di-did-dle-um,

Leader
F

Group
C7   F   C7   F

Go 'round the moun-tain;
Swing 'round your part - ner;
Back 'round the moun-tain;
Girls through the win - dow;
Boys through the win - dow;
Find you a new love;

} To-di-did-dle-um, To-di-did-dle-um-dum.

Frère Jacques
Are You Sleeping?

French Folk Song
Traditional English Words

French: Frè - re Jac - ques, Frè - re Jac - ques,
Pronunciation: frɛ rə ʒa kə frɛ rə ʒa kə
English: Are you sleep - ing, are you sleep - ing,

Dor - mez - vous, dor - mez - vous?
dɔr me vu dɔr me vu
Broth - er John, Broth - er John?

Son - nez les ma - ti - nes, son - nez les ma - ti - nes,
sɔ ne le ma ti nə sɔ ne le ma ti nə
Morn-ing bells are ring - ing, morn-ing bells are ring - ing,

Din, dan, don, din, dan, don.
dɛ̃ dã dɔ̃ dɛ̃ dã dɔ̃
Ding, ding, dong, ding, ding, dong.

¡Que llueva!
It's Raining!

Mexican Children's Game Song

Spanish: 1.–2. Que llue - va, que llue - va, la ra - na es - tá en la
Pronunciation: 1.–2. ke ywe βa ke ywe βa la ɾa naes taen la
English: 1.–2. It's rain - ing, it's rain - ing, the frog is in the

cue - va; los pa - ja - ri - tos can - tan, la lu - na se le -
kwe βa los pa xa ɾi tos kan tan la lu na se le
cave, And the par - a - keets are sing - ing, the sil - ver moon is

van - ta. Que sí, que no!
βan ta ke si ke no
ris - ing. Oh, yes! Oh, no!

1. Que cai - ga un cha - pa - rron.
ke kai gaun cha pa ɾon
The rain is fall - ing down.

2. Le can - ta el la - bra - dor.
le kan tael la βɾa ðoɾ
The farm - er sings the song.

EL FLORON

THE FLOWER

Mexican Game Song
English Version by MMH

do

			D			G			D			

Spanish: El flo - rón es - tá en las ma - nos, Y en las

Pronunciation: el flo ɾon es ta en las ma nos yen las

English: In my hand is a love - ly flow - er, Pret - ty

D A7 D G

ma - nos es - tá el flo - rón. A - di - vi - nen quién lo

ma nos es ta el flo ɾon a ði βi neng kyen lo

flow - er I hold in my hand. Now, I won - der who will

D A7 D

tie - ne, O se que - da de plan - tón.

tye ne o se ke ða ðe plan ton

have it, Or will it stay in my hand?

BUILT MY LADY A FINE BRICK HOUSE

Texas Folk Song

Built my la-dy a fine brick house, Built it in a gar-den;

I put her in but she jumped out, So fare thee well my dar-lin'!

Juan Pirulero

New Mexican Folk Song

Spanish: Es - te es el jue - go de Juan Pi - ru - le - ro;
Pronunciation: es tes el xwe go ðe xwɑn pi ɾu le ɾo
English: This is the game ___ of Juan Pi - ru - le - ro;

Que ca - da quien a - tien - da a su jue - go.
ke kɑ ða kyen ɑ tyen dɑ su xwe go
Eve - ry - one lis - ten, learn how to play it.

Au clair de la lune
IN THE MOONLIGHT

French Folk Song
English Version by MMH

G   D7   G   D7

French: **Au clair de la   lu - ne,   Mon a - mi Pier - rot,**
Pronunciation: o klɛr də la   lü   nə   mɔ̃ na   mi pyɛ   ro
English: **Out here in the   moon-light,   My good friend Pier - rot,**

G   D7   G   D7   G

Prê - te moi ta   plu - me,   Pour é - crire un   mot.
prɛ   tə mwa ta   plü mə   pu rɛ kri rœ̃   mo
Look now, my poor   can - dle   Will not ev - en   glow.

Am   A7   D7

Ma chan-delle est   mor - te,   Je n'ai plus de   feu;
mã shã də lɛ   mɔr tə   ʒə ne plü də   fö
I must write a   let - ter,   Help me, I im - plore!

G   D7   G   D7   G

Ou - vre moi ta   por - te,   Pour l'a - mour de   Dieu.
u   vrə mwa ta   pɔr   tə   pur la mur də   dyö
For the love of   hea - ven,   Op - en up your   door!

AIKEN DRUM

Scottish Folk Song

Verse

1. There ___ was a man lived in the moon, lived
2. And his hat was made of good cream cheese, of
3. And his coat was made of good roast beef, of
4. And his but-tons were made of pen - ny loaves, of
5. And his breech-es were made of hag - gis bags, of

in the moon, lived in the moon.
good cream cheese, of good cream cheese,
good roast beef, of good roast beef,
pen - ny loaves, of pen - ny loaves,
hag - gis bags, of hag - gis bags,

There ___ was a man lived in the moon,
And his hat was made of good cream cheese,
And his coat was made of good roast beef,
And his but-tons were made of pen - ny loaves,
And his breech-es were made of hag - gis bags,

And his name was Ai - ken Drum.

Refrain

And he played u - pon a la - dle, a la - dle, a la - dle,

And he played u - pon a la - dle, And his name was Ai-ken Drum.

Ezekiel Saw the Wheel

African American Spiritual

E - ze - kiel ___ saw ___ the wheel,

'way up in the mid - dle of the air.

E - ze - kiel ___ saw ___ the wheel,

'way in the mid - dle of the air.

Sing All Along My Way

African American Spiritual

Oh! I'm gon-na sing, gon-na sing, gon-na sing, gon-na

sing all a-long my way! Oh! I'm gon-na sing, gon-na

sing, gon-na sing, gon-na sing all a-long my way!

KASILYIO
The Wet Sage

Luiseño Lullaby

| Luiseño: | Ka | sil | yi | o____ | pe | ne | wi | ke | pe | ne | wi | ke | eu |
| Pronunciation: | kɑ | sɪl | yɪ | o | pɛ | nɛ | wɪ | kɛ | pɛ | nɛ | wɪ | kɛ | ɛu |

| Ka | sil | yi | o____ | pe | ne | wi | ke | pe | ne | wi | ke | eu | eu | eu |
| kɑ | sɪl | yɪ | o | pɛ | nɛ | wɪ | kɛ | pɛ | nɛ | wɪ | kɛ | ɛu | ɛu | ɛu |

Mama Paquita

Brazilian Carnival Song
English Version by Merrill Staton

1. Ma - ma Pa - qui - ta,   Ma - ma Pa - qui - ta,
2. Ma - ma Pa - qui - ta,   Ma - ma Pa - qui - ta,

Ma - ma Pa - qui - ta has no mon - ey for pa - pa - yas;
Ma - ma Pa - qui - ta has no mon - ey for pa - ja - mas;

Can't buy pa - pa - yas,   can't buy ba - nan - as;
Can't buy pa - ja - mas,   can't buy som - bre - ros;

She can - not buy pa - pa - yas or ba - nan - as. No, ma - ma - ma -
She can - not buy pa - ja - mas or som - bre - ros. No, ma - ma - ma -

ma, Ma - ma Pa - qui - ta,   Ma - ma Pa - qui - ta,
ma, Ma - ma Pa - qui - ta,   Ma - ma Pa - qui - ta,

Ma - ma Pa - qui - ta will not have a ripe pa - pa - ya;
Ma - ma Pa - qui - ta will not have the fine pa - ja - mas;

No ripe pa - pa - ya,   no ripe ba - nan - a,
No fine pa - ja - mas,   no fine som - bre - ros,

So go to Car - ni - val to laugh and dance and sing.

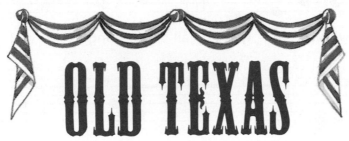

OLD TEXAS

Oklahoma Cowboy Song

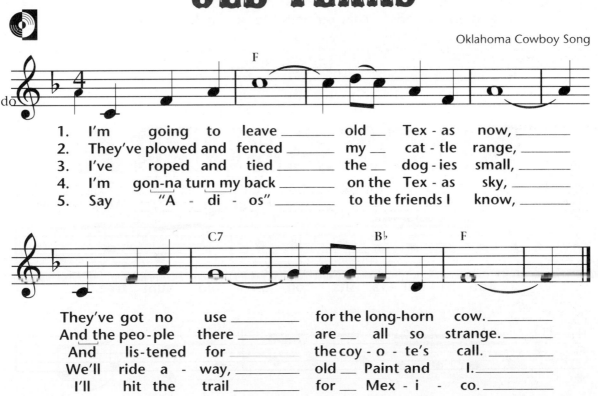

do

1. I'm   going to leave _____ old __ Tex - as now, _____
2. They've plowed and fenced _____ my __ cat - tle range, _____
3. I've   roped and tied _____ the __ dog - ies small, _____
4. I'm   gon-na turn my back _____ on the Tex - as sky, _____
5. Say   "A - di - os" _____ to the friends I know, _____

They've got no use _____ for the long-horn cow. _____
And the peo - ple there _____ are __ all so strange. _____
And lis-tened for _____ the coy - o - te's call. _____
We'll ride a - way, _____ old __ Paint and I. _____
I'll hit the trail _____ for __ Mex - i - co. _____

Chatter with the Angels

African American Spiritual

Chat-ter with the an - gels soon in the morn - ing,

Chat-ter with the an - gels all day long. I hope to

join that band and chat-ter with the an - gels all day long.

KOOKABURRA

Australian Round
Words by M. Sinclair

Koo - ka - bur - ra sits on an old gum tree. _____

Mer - ry, mer - ry king of the bush is he. _____

Laugh, Koo-ka-bur-ra, laugh, Koo-ka-bur-ra, Gay your life must be.

Old Tar River

American Folk Song

Moderato

1. Way __ down in North Car' - lin - a, *Whistle*
2. My old dog he won't go with me,
3. Rac-coon, Pos - sum had a fray, __
4. Old dog watch, smelled all a - round, __
5. Di - nah, I am going to leave you;

On the banks of Old Tar Riv - er, *Whistle*
He'd rath-er hunt far's I can see. __
Fought all night un - til next day, __
Found Rac - coon just left the ground, __
When I'm gone don't let it grieve you,

Go from there to Al - a - bam - a, *Whistle*
He smells some-thing up the hill, __
When day broke went Poss' to the hol-low,
Then he bark right up the tree, __
First to the win - dow, then to the door, __

For to see my old Aunt Han-nah. *Whistle*
If I don't find it, he sure will. __
Rac-coon says, "I bet - ter fol-low."
Rac-coon says, "You can't catch me." __
Look-ing for to see my ban - jo.

WHO BUILT THE ARK?

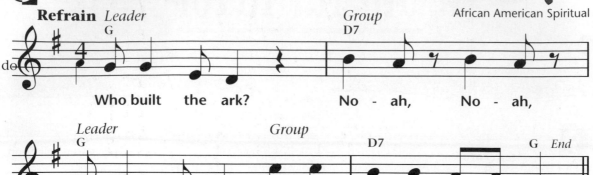

African American Spiritual

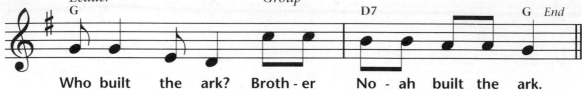

Refrain *Leader*   *Group*

Who built the ark?   No - ah,   No - ah,

Leader   *Group*   *End*

Who built the ark? Broth - er No - ah built the ark.

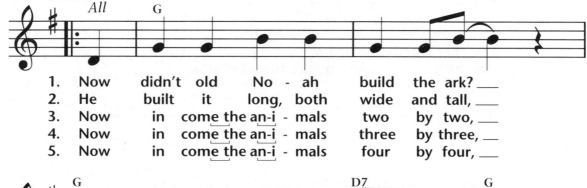

Verse *All*

1. Now didn't old No - ah build the ark? ___
2. He built it long, both wide and tall, ___
3. Now in come the an-i - mals two by two, ___
4. Now in come the an-i - mals three by three, ___
5. Now in come the an-i - mals four by four, ___

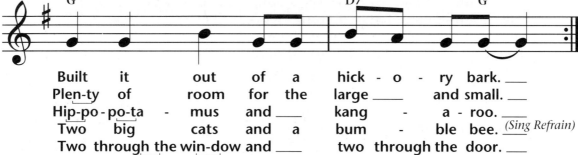

Built it out of a hick - o - ry bark. ___
Plen-ty of room for the large ___ and small. ___
Hip-po-po-ta - mus and ___ kang - a - roo. ___
Two big cats and a bum - ble bee. *(Sing Refrain)*
Two through the win-dow and ___ two through the door. ___

Now in come the animals. . .

6. . . . five by five, Four little sparrows and the redbird's wife,

7. . . . six by six, Elephant laughed at the monkey's tricks,

8. . . . seven by seven, Four from home and the rest from heaven.*

9. . . . eight by eight, Some were on time and the others were late,

10. . . . nine by nine, Some was a-shouting and some was a-crying.

11. . . . ten by ten, Five black roosters and five black hens,

12. Now Noah says, "Go shut that door, The rain's started dropping and we can't take more."*

*Sing refrain after verses 4, 8 and 12 only.

Alouette

French Canadian Folk Song

Refrain

French: A - lou - et - te, gen - tille a - lou - et - te,
Pronunciation: a lw ɛ tə ʒɑ̃ ti ya lw ɛ tə

End (Fine)

A - lou - et - te, je te plu - me - rai.
a lw ɛ tə ʒə tə plü mə ɾɛ

Verse

Leader   Group

1. Je te plu - me-rai la tête,   Je te plu - me-rai la tête,
   ʒə tə plü mə ɾɛ la tɛt ʒə tə plü mə ɾɛ la tɛt
2. Je te plu - me-rai le bec,   Je te plu - me-rai le bec,
   ʒə tə plü mə ɾɛ lə bɛk ʒə tə plü mə ɾɛ lə bɛk

Go back to the beginning and sing to the end (Da Capo al Fine)

Leader   Group   No repeat first time

1. Et la tête, et la tête.   A - lou-ette, a - lou-ette. Uh!
   e la tɛt e la tɛt a lw ɛt a lw ɛt o
2. Et le bec, et le bec.
   e lə bɛk e lə bɛk
   Et la tête, et la tête.
   e la tɛt e la tɛt

3. **Le nez** lə ne

4. **Le dos** lə do

5. **Les pattes** le pat

6. **Le cou** lə ku

THE FOX

English Folk Song

Freely

F

1. The fox went out on a chill-y night,
2. He ran till he came to a great big bin,
3. He grabbed the gray goose by the neck;
4. Then old Mo-ther Flip-per-Flop-per jumped out of bed.
5. Then John he went to the top of the hill;

F   C7

He prayed for the moon for to give him light,
Where the ducks and the geese were put there-in.
Threw a duck a-cross his back.
Out of the win-dow she cocked her head,
Blew his horn both loud and shrill;

F

For he'd man-y a mile to
"A cou-ple of you will
He did-n't mind their
Cry-ing, "John, John! The
The fox he said, "I'd bet-ter

Bb   F   C7

go that night a-fore he reached the
grease my chin a-fore I leave this
quack, quack, quack And their legs all dang-ling
gray goose is gone And the fox is on the
flee with my kill Or they'll soon be on my

334

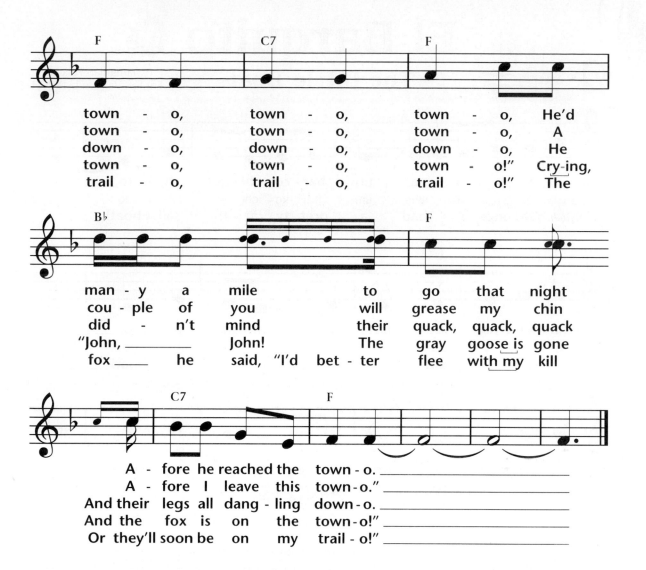

town - o, town - o, town - o, He'd
town - o, town - o, town - o, A
down - o, down - o, down - o, He
town - o, town - o, town - o!" Cry-ing,
trail - o, trail - o, trail - o!" The

man - y a mile to go that night
cou - ple of you will grease my chin
did - n't mind their quack, quack, quack
"John, _____ John! The gray goose is gone
fox _____ he said, "I'd bet - ter flee with my kill

A - fore he reached the town - o. _____
A - fore I leave this town-o." _____
And their legs all dang - ling down-o. _____
And the fox is on the town-o!" _____
Or they'll soon be on my trail - o!" _____

6. He ran till he came to his cozy den,
   There were the little ones, eight, nine, ten.
   They said, "Daddy, better go back again
   'Cause it must be a mighty fine town-o, town-o, town-o!"
   They said, "Daddy, . . ."

7. Then the fox and his wife without any strife,
   Cut up the goose with a fork and knife;
   They never had such a supper in their life
   And the little ones chewed on the bones-o, bones-o, bones-o.
   They never had . . .

El Barquito
The Little Boat

Panamanian Folk Song
English Version by MMH

Spanish: Ha - bía u-na vez un bar - co chi - qui - ti - to, _____
Pronunciation: a βyau na βes um baɾ ko chi ki ti to
English: Oh, once I had a pret - ty lit - tle sail - boat! _____

ha - bía u-na vez un bar - co chi - qui - ti - to, _____
a βyau na βes um baɾ ko chi ki ti to
Oh, once I had a pret - ty lit - tle sail - boat!

ha - bía u-na vez un bar - co chi - qui - ti - to, _____
a βyau na βes um baɾ ko chi ki ti to
Oh, once I had a pret - ty lit - tle sail - boat!

Que no po - dí - a, que no po - dí - a,
ke no po ði a ke no po ði a
A - las, it could not, a - las, it could not,

que no po - dí - a na - ve - gar.
ke no po ði a na βe gar
a - las, it could not go to sea!

Pa - sa - ron u - na, dos, tres, cua - tro, cin - co,
pa sa ron u na ðos tres kwa tro sing ko
Well it was one, two, three, four, five, six, sev - en,

336

There's a Little Wheel A-Turnin'

African American Folk Song

1. There's a lit-tle wheel __ a-turn-in' in my heart.
2. There's a lit-tle bell __ a-ring-in' in my heart.
3. There's a lit-tle song __ a-sing-in' in my heart.

There's a lit-tle wheel __ a-turn-in' in my heart.
There's a lit-tle bell __ a-ring-in' in my heart.
There's a lit-tle song __ a-sing-in' in my heart.

In my heart, _____ in my heart. _____

There's a lit-tle wheel __ a-turn-in' in my heart.
There's a lit-tle bell __ a-ring-in' in my heart.
There's a lit-tle song __ a-sing-in' in my heart.

My
Good Old Man

Southern American Folk Song

1. Where are you go - ing,
2. What will you buy there,
3. Bush - el will kill you, } my good old man?
4. What for to die, ___
5. Why will you haunt me,

Where are you go - ing,
What will you buy there,
Bush - el will kill you, } my sug - ar, my lamb?
What for to die, ___
Why will you haunt me,

Best old man in the world. _____

*Spoken:
(1) To market.
(2) Bushel of eggs.
(3) Don't care if it does.
(4) So I can haunt you.
(5) So I can always be near you.

THE
Kindergarten Wall

Words and Music by J. McCutcheon

Freely

Verse

1. When I was a lit - tle kid   not so long a - go,
(2.) first, ___ sec - ond, third ___ grade,   fourth ___ grade, ___ too,
3. Late - ly I've been wor - ried as I   look a-round and see,

I   had to learn a lot of stuff I   did - n't ev - en know:
Where   I had to learn the big ___ things the   big ___ kids ___ do:
An   aw - ful lot of grown-ups act - ing   fool - ish as can be.

How to dress my - self and tie my shoes,   how to jump a rope,
To ___ add, sub - tract, and mult - i - ply,   read and write and play,
Now I know there's lots of things to know I   have-n't mas-tered yet,

How to smile   for a pic - ture with-out look - ing like a dope.
How to sit in a lit-tle un-com-fort-a-ble desk for near - ly half a day.
But it seems there's real im - por - tant stuff that grown-ups soon for-get.

But of all the things I learned, my   fav'-rite of them all,
But of all the things they taught me, of   all the great and small,
So I'm sure we'd all be bet - ter off if   we would just re - call

340

Was a lit - tle poem hang - ing on the kin - der - gar - ten wall:
Still my fav' - rite was the po - em on the kin - der - gar - ten wall:
That ___ lit - tle poem hang - ing on the kin - der - gar - ten wall:

Refrain

Of all you learn here, re - mem - ber this the best:

Don't hurt each oth - er and clean up your mess;

Take a nap ev' - ry day, wash be - fore you eat,

Hold hands, stick to - geth - er, look be - fore you cross the street;

And re - mem - ber the seed in the lit - tle pa - per cup,

First the root goes down and then the plant grows up. 2. Was

Hop Up, My Ladies

Virginia Folk Song

Verse

C

1. Did you ev - er go to meet-ing, Un-cle Joe, Un-cle Joe?
2. Will your horse ___ car - ry dou - ble, Un-cle Joe, Un-cle Joe?
3. Is your horse a sin - gle-foot - er, Un-cle Joe, Un-cle Joe?
4. Say, ___ don't you want to gal - lop, Un-cle Joe, Un-cle Joe?
5. Say, you might ___ take a tum - ble, Un-cle Joe, Un-cle Joe?

C   G7

Did you ev - er go to meet-ing, Un - cle Joe? ___
Will your horse ___ car - ry dou - ble, Un - cle Joe? ___
Is your horse a sin - gle - foot - er, Un - cle Joe? ___
Say, ___ don't you want to gal - lop, Un - cle Joe? ___
Say, you might ___ take a tum - ble, Un - cle Joe? ___

C

Did you ev - er go to meet-ing, Un - cle Joe, Un - cle Joe?
Will your horse ___ car - ry dou - ble, Un - cle Joe, Un - cle Joe?
Is your horse a sin - gle-foot - er, Un - cle Joe, Un - cle Joe?
Say, ___ don't you want to gal - lop, Un - cle Joe, Un - cle Joe?
Say, you might ___ take a tum - ble, Un - cle Joe, Un - cle Joe?

F   G7   C

Don't mind the weath - er, so the wind don't blow.

Refrain

Hop up, my la-dies, three in a row, Hop up, my la-dies,

three in a row, Hop up, my la-dies, three in a row,

Don't mind the weath - er, so the wind don't blow.

American Song

1. Who's got a fish-pole? We do. Who's got a fish-pole? We do.
2. Who's got a line? ___ We do. Who's got a line? ___ We do.
3. Who's got a hook? ___ We do. Who's got a hook? ___ We do.

Who's got a fish-pole? We do. Fish-pole needs a line.
Who's got a line? ___ We do. Line ___ needs a hook.
Who's got a hook? ___ We do. Hook ___ needs a worm.

One Bottle of POP

Traditional English Round

One bot-tle o' pop, Two bot-tle o' pop,

Three bot-tle o' pop, Four bot-tle o' pop, Five bot-tle o' pop,

Six bot-tle o' pop, Sev-en bot-tle o' pop, Pop!

Don't chuck your muck in my dust-bin, my dust-bin, my dust-bin,

Don't chuck your muck in my dust-bin, my dust-bin's full.

Fish and chips and vin-e-gar, vin-e-gar, vin-e-gar,

Fish and chips and vin-e-gar, Vin-e-gar and Pop!

OLD PAINT

American Folk Song
Arranged by Mary Goetze

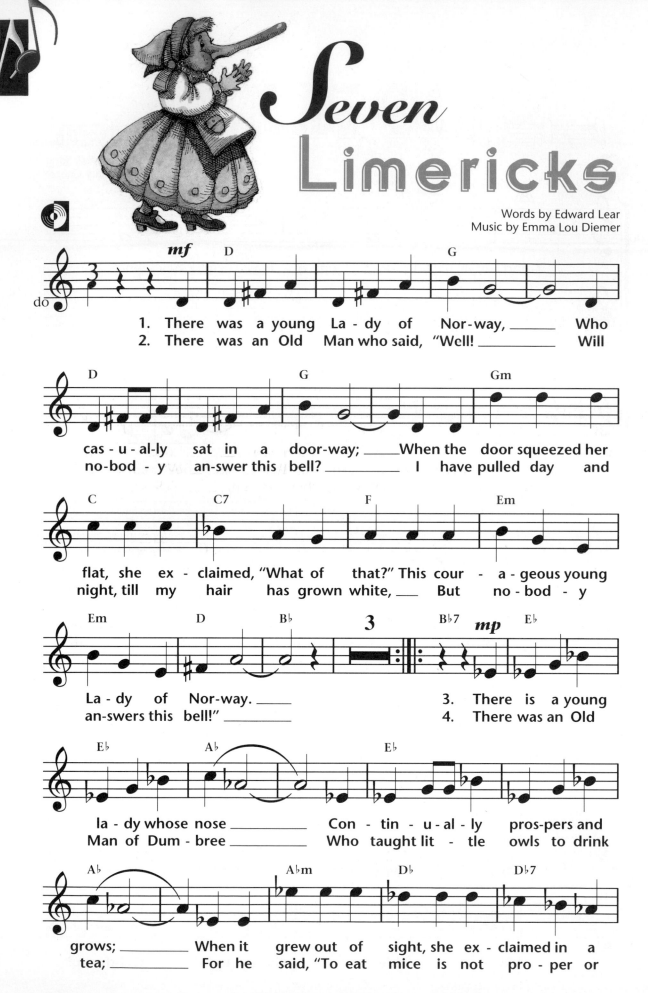

Seven Limericks

Words by Edward Lear
Music by Emma Lou Diemer

mf — D — G

1. There was a young La-dy of Nor-way, _____ Who
2. There was an Old Man who said, "Well! _____ Will

D — G — Gm

cas-u-al-ly sat in a door-way; _____When the door squeezed her
no-bod-y an-swer this bell? _____ I have pulled day and

C — C7 — F — Em

flat, she ex-claimed, "What of that?" This cour - a-geous young
night, till my hair has grown white, ___ But no-bod-y

Em — D — B♭ — **3** — B♭7 *mp* — E♭

La-dy of Nor-way. _____
an-swers this bell!" _____

3. There is a young
4. There was an Old

E♭ — A♭ — E♭

la-dy whose nose _____ Con-tin-u-al-ly pros-pers and
Man of Dum-bree _____ Who taught lit-tle owls to drink

A♭ — A♭m — D♭ — D♭7

grows; _____ When it grew out of sight, she ex-claimed in a
tea; _____ For he said, "To eat mice is not pro-per or

346

fright, "Oh! Fare - well to the   end of my nose!" _____
nice," ___ That am-i-ca-ble   Man of Dum-bree. _____

mf

5.   There was an old per - son   on Ware, _____ Who rode   on the
6.   There was a young la - dy   of Bute, _____ Who played on a
7.   There was an Old Man who, when lit - tle, _____ Fell   cas - u-al-ly

back of   a   bear, ___ When they asked, "Does it trot?" He said, "Cer-tain - ly
sil - ver-gilt flute; _____   She played sev-eral jigs   to her un - cle's white
in - to   a   ket-tle __   But grow - ing too stout he could nev - er   get

1., 2.

not! He's a   Mopp - si - kon Flopp-si-kin bear!" _____
pigs: That a - mus - ing young la - dy of Bute. _____
out, So he   passed all   his

3.

life in that   ket - tle! _____

ALPINE SONG

Austrian Yodeling Song
Words Adapted by Susan Van Dyck

1.–4. Oh, an Aus-trian went yo-del-ing on a moun-tain so high.

(1.) When a - long came an a - va-lanche in-ter-rupt-ing his cry.
(2.) When a - long came a Saint Ber-nard in-ter-rupt-ing his cry.
(3.) When a - long came a Guern-sey cow in-ter-rupt-ing his cry.
(4.) When a - long came a Mar - tian in-ter-rupt-ing his cry.

Refrain

Yo - lay - dee, yo - de-lay-hee-hee, Oh yo - de-lay-hee-hoo.

Yo - de - lay - hee - hee, Oh yo - de lay - hee - hoo.

Yo - de - lay - hee - hee, Oh yo - de - lay - hee - hoo.

Yo - de - lay - hee - hoo - oh lay.

Insert on each verse as follows:

1. shh-shh . . .

2. pant-pant, shh-shh . . .

3. moo-moo, pant-pant, shh-shh . . .

4. beep-beep, moo-moo, pant-pant, shh-shh . . .

Oma Rapeti
Run, Rabbit

New Zealand Folk Song
Collected and Transcribed by Kathy B. Sorensen

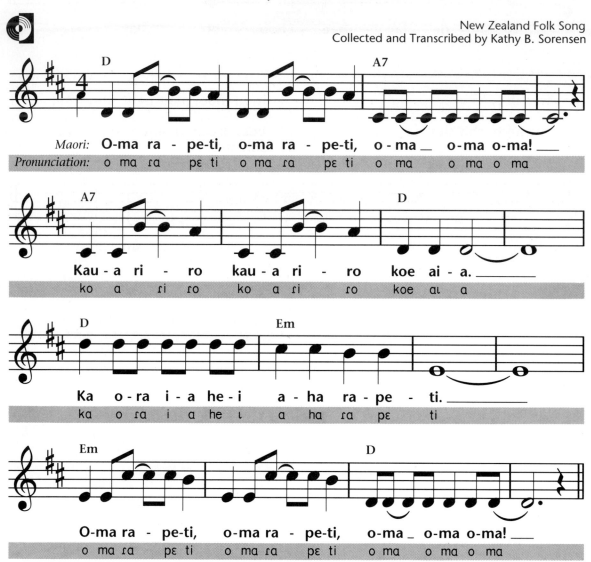

Maori: O-ma ra - pe-ti, o-ma ra - pe-ti, o-ma __ o-ma o-ma! __
Pronunciation: o ma ɾa pɛ ti o ma ɾa pɛ ti o ma o ma o ma

Kau - a ri - ro kau-a ri - ro koe ai - a. __
ko a ɾi ɾo ko a ɾi ɾo koe ɑ a

Ka o-ra i-a he-i a-ha ra-pe - ti. __
ka o ɾa i a he ɪ a ha ɾa pɛ ti

O-ma ra - pe-ti, o-ma ra - pe-ti, o-ma __ o-ma o-ma! __
o ma ɾa pɛ ti o ma ɾa pɛ ti o ma o ma o ma

350

English: Run, rab - bit, run, rab - bit, run, run, run!

Don't give _ the far - mer _ his fun, fun, fun.

He'll get by with - out his rab-bit ___ pie,

so run, rab - bit, run, rab - bit, run, run, run!

The Old Brass Wagon

Midwestern American Singing Game

1. Cir - cle to the left,
2. Cir - cle to the right,
3. El - bow ___ swing,
4. Pro - me - nade ___ right, } the old brass wag - on,
5. Cen - ter ___ all,
6. Ev' - ry - bod - y swing,

Cir - cle to the left,
Cir - cle to the right,
El - bow ___ swing,
Pro - me - nade ___ right, } the old brass wag - on,
Out ___ to the ring,
Ev' - ry - bod - y swing,

Cir - cle to the left,
Cir - cle to the right,
El - bow ___ swing,
Pro - me - nade ___ right, } the old brass wag - on,
Cen - ter ___ all,
Ev' - ry - bod - y swing,

You're the one, my dar - ling.

352

TELEPHONE SONG

American Singing Game

Solo 1 D Bm *Solo 2* D7 A
"Hey, Char - ley!" _____ "I think I hear my name!" _

Solo 1 D Bm *Solo 2* D7 A
"Hey, Char - ley!" _____ "I think I hear it a - gain!"

Solo 1 D Bm D7 A
"You're want - ed on the tel - e - phone!"

Solo 2 D Bm D7 A
"If it is - n't Ma - ry I'm not ___ at home!"

Chorus D
With a rick - tick - tick - e - ty tick, _____ Oh yeah! __

A D A7 D
With a rick - tick - tick - e - ty tick, _____ Oh yeah.

OH, SUSANNA

Words and Music by Stephen Foster

Verse

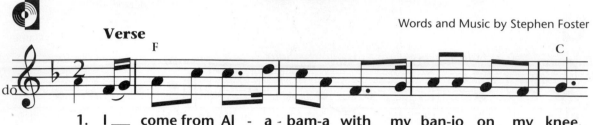

1. I __ come from Al - a - bam-a with   my ban-jo on   my knee.
2. I __ had   a dream the oth-er night, when ev'-ry-thing was   still.

I'm __ going to Loui-si - an - a, my __ true love for   to   see.
I __ thought I saw Su - san - na   a - com-ing down the   hill.

It __ rained all   night the   day I   left,   the weath-er it was   dry,
The __ buck-wheat cake was   in her mouth, the   tear was in her   eye.

The __ sun so   hot I   froze to death, Su - san-na, don't you   cry.
Says __   I, "I'm com-ing from the South, Su - san-na, don't you   cry."

Refrain

Oh,   Su - san - na,   oh,   don't you   cry for   me.

I __ come from Al - a - bam-a with my ban-jo on my   knee.

354

FOUR IN A BOAT

Lively *(Verse 3: Slowly)*

American Singing Game

1. Four in a boat and the tide runs high,
2. Choose your ___ part - ner and stay all day,
3. Eight in a boat and it won't go 'round,

Four in a boat and the tide runs high,
Choose your ___ part - ner and stay all day,
Eight in a boat and it won't go 'round,

1., 2.

Four in a boat and the tide runs high,
Choose your ___ part - ner and stay all day,
Eight in a boat and it

Wait-ing for my pret - ty one to come by and by.
We ___ don't ___ care ___ what the old folk ___ say.

3.

won't go 'round, And it sank to the bot-tom of the sea.

You're Invited
VIOLIN RECITAL

What do you see in this picture?

A **recital** is a concert given by a solo musician. A soloist usually performs with some kind of accompaniment, like a piano. The soloist has studied and practiced, and would like to share his or her work with others. Friends, family, and other music lovers may attend the recital.

A longer recital may have an **intermission.** An intermission is a short break between the selections of a concert. At intermission, the audience may stretch their legs, eat snacks, or chat with friends.

LISTEN to a violin recital.

LISTENING

CARNEGIE HALL

VIOLIN RECITAL
Presented by Midori

Caprice in A Minor
(excerpts)
by Niccolò Paganini

INTERMISSION

**Sonata No. 8
for Violin and Piano**
Allegro vivace
by Ludwig van Beethoven

Show your appreciation by clapping. Is this the same way you would show your appreciation at a baseball game? Why?

Listening

Some of the music listed below is very old, and some is new. Which type of music would you like to learn more about?

El grillo
JOSQUIN DES PREZ
1504

Minuet in G
from *Notebook for Anna Magdalena Bach*
CHRISTIAN PETZOLD
1725

Eine Kleine Nachtmusik
First Movement
WOLFGANG AMADEUS MOZART
1787

Discoveries

Clair de lune
from *Suite bergamasque*
CLAUDE DEBUSSY
1905

Cortège
LILI BOULANGER
1914

"Classical" Symphony
Third Movement
SERGEI PROKOFIEV
1917

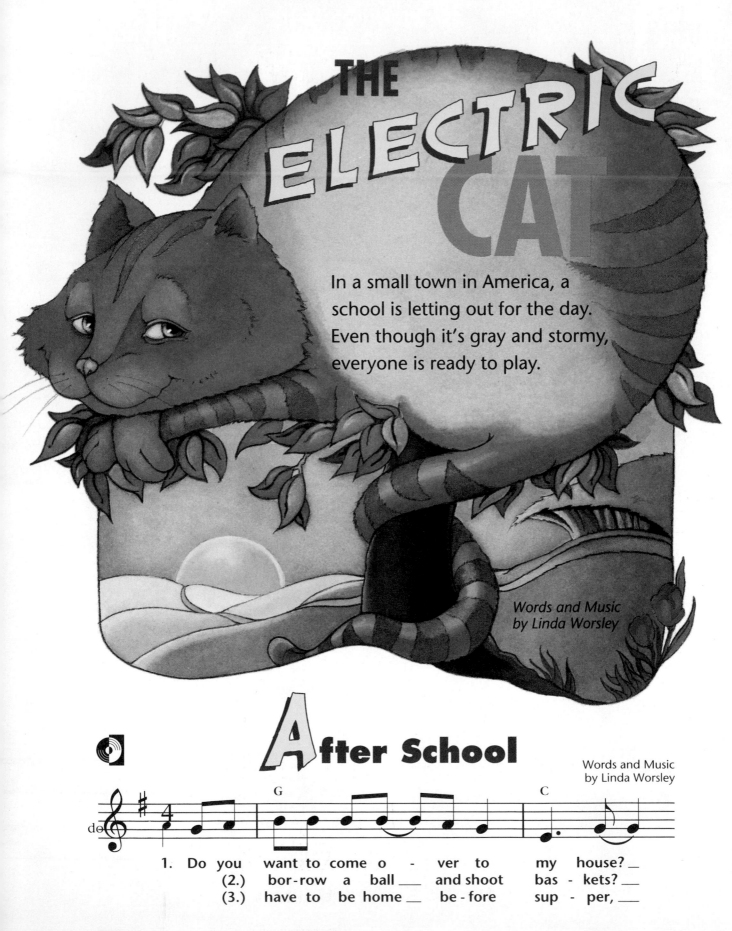

THE ELECTRIC CAT

In a small town in America, a school is letting out for the day. Even though it's gray and stormy, everyone is ready to play.

Words and Music by Linda Worsley

After School

Words and Music
by Linda Worsley

1. Do you want to come o - ver to my house? _
(2.) bor-row a ball __ and shoot bas - kets? __
(3.) have to be home __ be - fore sup - per, __

Do you   want to come o - ver and   play?
Can we   play with some vi - de-o   games?
And I   have to be home __ be-fore   dark,

There's a   tree we can climb, _ and   plen-ty of time _ af-ter
There's a   puz-zle to make, _ We'll eat ap-ples and cake _ af-ter
It's a   time we can play, _ the best time of the day _ af-ter

1. school.   2. Can I   school.   8   3. Well, I

3. school.   Come o - ver af-ter   school, Come on! __

Come o - ver af-ter   school!   O   K!

While the other children make their afternoon plans, Shawn—the new girl in town—walks home alone. Her parents don't understand why she is so down.

Lonely and sad, Shawn can't help wishing she had never left her friends in Springville.

All I Need Is a Friend

Words and Music
by Linda Worsley

Wistfully

Shawn: Moth-er says I need more vi-ta-mins, I don't think so. ____

Fa-ther says I need more ex-er-cise, I don't think so. ____ I

just need some-one I can talk with, walk with, play with,

spend the day with. I don't think so. I know so.

a tempo

Teach-er says I need more con-fi-dence, but I can't pre-

Mother *Father* *Teacher*

tend. She needs vi-ta-mins, She needs ex-er-cise. She needs

Shawn

con-fi-dence, All I need is a friend.

Shawn's one and only friend is good old Hairy, her cat, who visits her on the porch. All of a sudden, an electrical storm blows in with a clap of thunder. Hairy's fur stands on end, and he bolts up the tallest tree in town! No matter what Shawn and her parents do, Hairy won't come down.

After the storm has passed, Sandy—a girl from school—walks by and asks, "Are you looking for something?" Shawn tells her the whole story.

My Cat's Gone Up in a Tree

Words and Music by Linda Worsley

The next day, Kurt gets into the act when he meets his friend Sandy after school. Kurt is really crabby. He's had three very bad days.

crab - by, crank-y and cross, I feel sulk - y, sul - len and

bos - sy, _____ and I have to say I like me that

1.

way, so I'm gon-na be crab - by all day! 2. Went

(2.) *Sandy:* **You**

2.

real-ly are crab-by! I'm gon-na be crab-by all day! _____

You're

Sandy and Kurt approach Shawn, still standing sadly by the tree. The three of them try to coax Hairy down with tuna fish– no luck!

The next day, they call the fire department, but the ladder isn't tall enough. A small crowd of schoolmates gathers at the foot of Shawn's tree. Shawn begins to feel better as the children sing this song.

Two Heads Are Better than One

Words and Music
by Linda Worsley

Freely

Sandy: 1. Two heads are bet-ter than one ____ When there's a job that
Two friends: 2. Three heads are bet-ter than two ____ When there's a lot you've

must be done, ____ yes, two heads are bet - ter than,
got to do, ____ yes, three heads are bet - ter than,

much bet - ter than one!
much bet - ter than two!

All

And now that there are four of us,

or five or six or more of us, it all de -

pends on wheth - er we can work to - geth - er.

First time, other friends
Second time, Sandy

Second time to Coda

When there's a puz-zle to solve, ____ when there's a prob-lem

to re-solve, ___ well, two heads are bet-ter than,

much bet-ter than . . . *"My grandmother says. . . ."*

Coda

to re-solve, _ or in a pre-di-ca-ment, when you're com-ing un-done,

Solo 1

Solo 2

you know that six heads are bet-ter than, five heads are bet-ter than,

Kurt

Sandy

four heads are bet-ter than, three heads are bet-ter than,

All

two heads are bet-ter than, much bet-ter than one! _ (bet-ter than one!)

Another storm blows in. Suddenly, there is a crack of thunder. Guess who jumps out of the tree and into Shawn's arms? Good old Hairy, of course, and his hair is standing on end like an electric cat's. Mother decides Hairy will be a house cat from now on as Shawn joins her new friends for a pizza celebration!

Two Friends Are Better Than One

Two friends are better than one,
When it's a time for having fun, yes,
Two friends are better than, much better than one!
Three friends are better than two,
When there's a lot you want to do, yes,
Three friends are better than, much better than two!
　And now that there are four of us,
　Or five or six or more of us,
　It all depends on whether
　We have fun together.
When there's a game to be played,
When there's a treehouse to be made, and
When it's a Saturday, and you want to have fun!
　You know that six friends are better than,
　Five friends are better than,
　Four friends are better than,
　Three friends are better than,
Two friends are better than,
Much better than one! (better than one!)

—Linda Worsley

The Goat Who Couldn't Sneeze

A Musical Play Based on a Mexican Folk Tale
Music by Juan Orrego-Salas Words by Mary Goetze

Far up in the Sierra Madre Mountains, there lived a herd of sneezing goats. Now, they weren't sick, mind you, and they didn't have allergies. These goats just loved to sneeze in the breeze!

Ah-choo!

Music by Juan Orrego-Salas
Words by Mary Goetze

We love to graze on our beau-ti-ful hill,

Third time, go to Coda **4** 1.

The grass is so thick we can eat our fill.

Our kids are con-tent as they romp in the breez-es,

Our peace is on-ly dis-turbed by our sneez-es.

Ah - choo!   Ah - choo!   Ah - choo!

We nev-er get colds, we have no al-ler-gies, But nev-er-the-less,

but nev-er-the-less, _____ We some-times sneeze, and

Go back **Coda**
to the beginning

sneeze, and sneeze. _____

Ah-choo!   Ah-choo!   Ahh - choo!   Ah-choo!   Ah-choo!

Ah - choo!   *(Individual sneezes)*   Ah - choo!

It's easy to sneeze. Everyone can do it! Everyone except for the great goat leader. He tried to sneeze, but he just couldn't. He was very embarrassed. "Why can everyone sneeze but me?" he wondered.

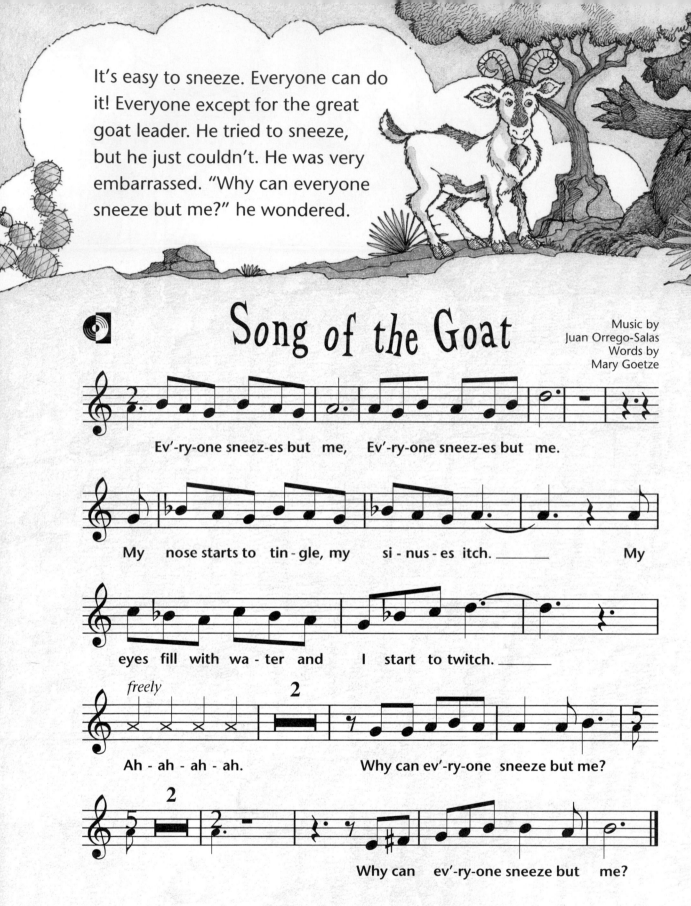

Song of the Goat

Music by
Juan Orrego-Salas
Words by
Mary Goetze

Ev'-ry-one sneez-es but me, Ev'-ry-one sneez-es but me.

My nose starts to tin-gle, my si-nus-es itch. _____ My

eyes fill with wa-ter and I start to twitch. _____

freely

Ah - ah - ah - ah. Why can ev'-ry-one sneeze but me?

Why can ev'-ry-one sneeze but me?

The goats tried to teach their leader to sneeze, but they couldn't. They invited all of the animals to a great meeting to teach the goat to sneeze.

The Bear and the Wildcat

Music by Juan Orrego-Salas
Words by Mary Goetze

A All

1. Let's go get our friend the bear,
2. Get the wild - cat he's our friend,
3. Let's go ask our friend the teach - er,
4. Get the doc - tor, ask the ques - tion,

Reprise

She will have a thought to share.   1. *Bear:*
He will have ad - vice to lend.   2. *Wildcat:*
Sure - ly she can help this crea - ture. 3. *Teacher:*
Sure - ly he'll have some sug - ges - tion. 4. *Doctor:*

B Solo

I don't see why you can't sneeze, Why you can't,

Why you can't.   Here's how to do it with ease:

Get   down on your knees, put your head in   the breeze,
You   wrin - kle your nose, and you   wait till one grows,
On a   day that is gust-y, find a   place that is dust-y,
There is no med - i - cine   that will help you   be - gin,

(1-3) Then it's   ah - ah - ah - ah - choo!
(4)   To go   ah - ah - ah - ah - choo!

The great goat tried everything, but nothing
worked. The other animals left him all alone.
Maybe someone in town could help.

Welcome Song

Music by Juan Orrego-Salas
Words by Mary Goetze

All **f**

Wel-come to you lit-tle goat. Wel-come to our lit-tle town.

(**mf** cresc.) **f**

Take a swim in our pool, join our chil-dren at school, where of

course there's no hors - ing a - round. _____

4 **f**

1.   Wel-come to you lit-tle goat.   Walk through our streets in good
2.   Wel-come to you lit-tle goat.   Walk on the bridge o'er the

health.   You can feel free to munch when it comes time for lunch, Just
brook.   You need have no fear, there's no troll liv-ing here, Now

don't make a pig of your - self. look. You
don't be too sheep-ish to

need have no fear, _____ There's no troll liv - ing here.

No one could help! Hungry and discouraged, he turned back toward the mountains. He walked and walked. When he came to a small patch of grass, he stopped to graze and rest. There, a strange buzzing sounded in his ear.

Song of the Bees

Music by
Juan Orrego-Salas
Words by
Mary Goetze

Work - er bees flut - ter near - by,

Buzz 'round his nose and his eyes,

Tick - le and tease him un - til he is sneez-ing,

Ah - ah - ah - ah - choo!

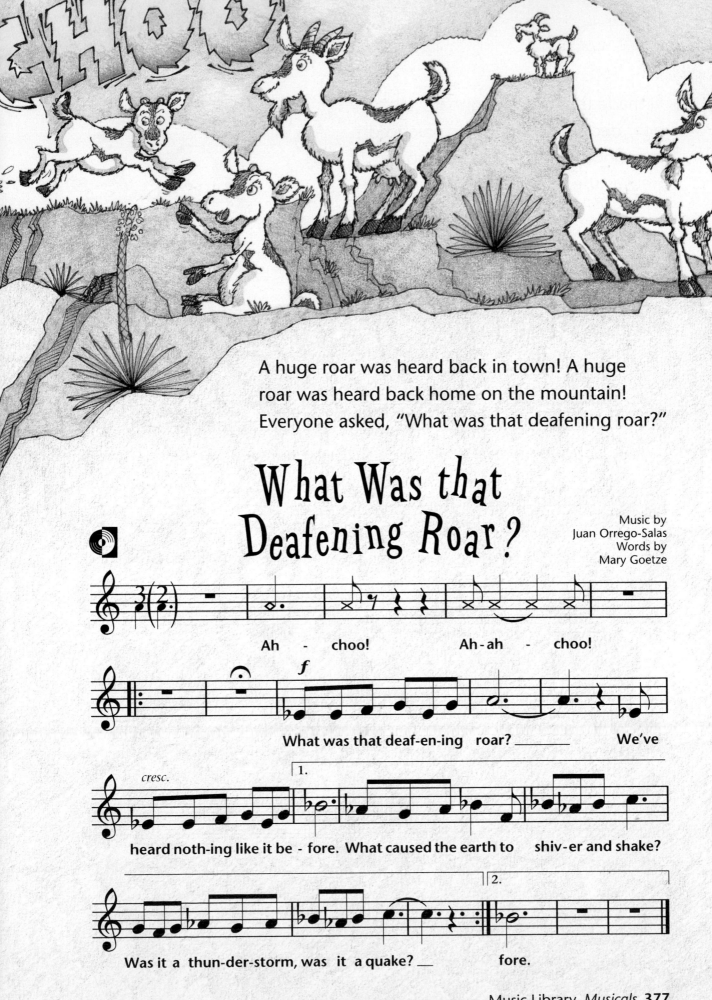

A huge roar was heard back in town! A huge roar was heard back home on the mountain! Everyone asked, "What was that deafening roar?"

What Was that Deafening Roar?

Music by
Juan Orrego-Salas
Words by
Mary Goetze

Ah - choo! Ah-ah - choo!

f

What was that deaf-en-ing roar? _____ We've

cresc.

1.

heard noth-ing like it be - fore. What caused the earth to shiv-er and shake?

2.

Was it a thun-der-storm, was it a quake? ___ fore.

"I made that deafening roar," the goat declared proudly. He practiced sneezing the rest of the way home. He was the happiest goat of all time!

I Made that Deafening Roar!

Music by
Juan Orrego-Salas
Words by Mary Goetze

Goat

I made that deaf-en-ing roar, ___ I've done noth-ing like it be - fore,

I with the gen-er-ous help of the bees, Was a - ble to sneeze an earth -

shat-ter-ing sneeze. Yes, it was I who sneezed. It was I! It was I!

5 *All*

The goat made that deaf-en-ing roar, _____ He's

Spoken

done noth-ing like it be - fore. Noth-ing like this, noth-ing but

noth-ing like this we've heard be-fore! Like this deaf-en-ing roar.

You Sneezed!

Music by
Juan Orrego-Salas
Words by
Mary Goetze

We're glad that you fi - nal - ly sneezed,

We could - n't be an - y - more pleased,

You sneezed! You sneezed! We're all so pleased!

Now look at him gig-gle and look at him grin.

*Go back to the beginning and
sing to the end (Da Capo al Fine)*

And don't an - y-one ask him to do it a - gain!

All the goats shared in their leader's happiness.
Since that day, mountain goats always sneeze
when they see bees.

GLOSSARY

A

accelerando   to get faster gradually, **60**

accompaniment   a musical background to a melody, **184**

Appalachian dulcimer   also known as a zither; a stringed instrument played with both hands: one hand plucks one of the three strings as the other holds or stops the strings near the end, **233**

B

ballet   a story told through dance and music, **10**

bar line (|)   a line that marks the end of a measure, **20**

C

canon   a piece of music in which the melody is introduced and then imitated one or more times; similar to a round, **77, 153**

cello   the second-largest instrument in the violin family. It is held between the knees and played by bowing or plucking the strings, **173, 230**

chord   three or more pitches sounded together, **187**

coda   an ending section to a piece of music, **160**

conduct   to lead performers using hands, **102**

crescendo (—◁)   to get louder gradually, **75**

D

decrescendo (▷—)   to get softer gradually, **75**

dotted half note (♩.)   a note equal to one half note plus one quarter note, **105**

dotted quarter note (♩.)   a note equal to one quarter note plus one eighth note, **189**

dotted quarter rest (𝄽·)   a rest equal to one quarter rest plus one eighth rest, **106**

double bass or bass   the largest instrument in the violin family. It is held upright and played by bowing or plucking the strings, **173, 212**

downbeat   the strong beat, **102**

dynamics   the loudness or softness of music, **34, 74**

E

eighth note (♪)   two eighth notes equal two sounds to a beat (♫), **20**

equal rhythm   two sounds of the same length to a beat, **94**

F

fermata (⌒)   a symbol placed over a note to show that it should be held longer than its normal value, **38**

fife and drum   an ensemble in which the fife, an instrument from the woodwind family, carries the melody as the drum, from the percussion family, provides the rhythm accompaniment, **114**

first ending ([1._____) a sign that tells you to go back to the beginning of the song and sing to the second ending, **236**

folk song a song that emerged from the culture of a group of people, usually of unknown authorship, **92**

forte (f) loud, **34**

G

guitar a popular member of the stringed instrument family; it has either six or twelve strings and is played by strumming, plucking, or picking, **164, 186–187**

H

half note (♩) a note that shows a sound that is two beats long, **63**

harp one of the oldest stringed instruments. The orchestral harp has a large, triangle-like frame that holds 46 strings and 7 pedals. It stands upright and is played by plucking or strumming the strings, **86–87**

heavier voice quality of singing or speaking that usually gives louder, fuller, and lower sound, **14**

I

intermission a short break between selections of a concert, **357**

introduction music that comes before a song or composition, **160**

L

ledger line an extra line added above or below the staff, **108**

legato smoothly, **221**

lighter voice quality of singing or speaking that gives quieter, generally higher sound, **14**

lute a stringed instrument with a pear-shaped back; it usually has 20 strings and, like the guitar, is played by strumming, plucking, or picking the strings, **198–199, 207**

M

marcato with extra force, **221**

mariachi a Mexican instrumental group that may include trumpets, violins, guitars, a guitarrón, a vihuela, and a small harp, **164–165**

measure a unit used to group notes and rests, **20**

melodic ostinato a short melody that repeats over and over, **119**

melody the tune; a series of pitches moving upward, downward, or staying the same, **8**

meter signature the symbol that tells how many beats are grouped in each measure and what kind of note equals one beat, **20**

O

orchestra a large group of instrumental performers, usually including four families of instruments: strings, woodwinds, brass, and percussion, **44–47**

ostinato a musical pattern that repeats over and over, **117, 136**

P

pentatonic having five pitches, **157**

pentatonic scale a five-tone scale, **157**

phrase a short section of music that is one musical thought, **139**

piano (*p*) soft, **34**

pitch the highness or lowness of a sound, **8, 26**

pitch syllable the name of a pitch, such as *do* or *re*, **29**

pizzicato short and light; played by plucking a stringed instrument, **212**

Q

quarter note (♩) a musical sign that shows one sound to a beat, **20**

quarter rest (𝄽) a musical sign that shows a beat with no sound, **20**

R

recital a concert given by a solo musician, **356**

recorder a small member of the woodwind family; it has eight finger holes and is played by blowing into a mouthpiece, **198, 207**

refrain a section of a song that is repeated after each verse, **54**

repeat one way a melody moves; staying on the same pitch, **142**

repeat sign (𝄇) a symbol that tells you to repeat part of a piece of music, **116**

rhythm combinations of longer and shorter sounds and silences, **3, 32**

rhythm pattern an organized group of long and short sounds that repeats, **5**

rondo a piece of music in which the A section always returns; the sections in between are different (A B A C A), **164**

S

scale a group of pitches in order from lowest to highest, **157**

scat a type of singing that began as singers imitated jazz instrument sounds; uses nonsense syllables sung in melodies, **246**

second ending (|2. ⌐) the ending after the first ending, **236**

sixteenth note (♪) four sixteenth notes equal one beat (𝅘𝅥𝅯𝅘𝅥𝅯𝅘𝅥𝅯𝅘𝅥𝅯), **146**

skip one way a melody moves; higher or lower jumping over one or more pitches, **142**

slur (⌒) a symbol that tells you to sing a syllable on more than one pitch, **108**

speech piece words set to a rhythm with no melody, **3**

spiritual an African American folk song, many of which began as religious songs, **110**

staccato short and light, **221**

staff the five lines and four spaces on which musical notes are written, **26**

step one way a melody moves; higher or lower to the next pitch, **142**

string family instruments such as violin, viola, cello, and double bass that are sounded by plucking or by drawing a bow across strings, **173**

synthesizer   an electronic instrument that can create sounds or imitate the tone colors of traditional instruments, **70**

T

tempo   the speed of the beat, **58**

tie ( )   a curved line that connects two notes of the same pitch and means that the sound should be held for the length of both notes, **63**

tonal center   the home tone or pitch around which a melody seems to center; often the last pitch, **224**

tone color   the special sound of each instrument or voice, **14**

treble clef or G clef ( )   tells that the notes on the second line of a staff are called G, **202**

U

unequal rhythm   two sounds of unequal lengths to a beat, **94**

upbeat   the weak beat before the downbeat, **102, 192–193**

V

verse   a section of a song that is repeated using the same melody but different words, **54**

viola   a stringed instrument slightly larger than the violin. It is held under the chin and played by bowing or plucking the strings, **173**

violin   the smallest instrument in the string family. It is held under the chin and played by bowing or plucking the strings, **47, 172–173, 230**

violoncello   see **cello**, **173, 230**

W

whole note (o)   a note to show a sound that lasts four beats, **190**

whole rest (▬)   a rest to show a silence that lasts four beats, **190**

CLASSIFIED INDEX

FOLK

HOLIDAYS, SEASONAL, PATRIOTIC

INDEX OF POETRY

INDEX OF LISTENING SELECTIONS

INTERVIEWS

INDEX OF SONGS AND SPEECH PIECES

from ALLIGATOR PIE, published by Macmillan of Canada, Copyright © 1974 Dennis Lee.

MMB Music, Inc. for *Oh Lord, I Want Two Wings* from CHATTER WITH THE ANGELS by Shirley McRae. © 1980 MMB Music, Inc., Saint Louis. Used by Permission. All Rights Reserved. For *Old Paint* and *The Old Sow's Hide* from THE CAT CAME BACK by Mary Goetze. © 1984 MMB Music, Inc., Saint Louis. Used by Permission. All Rights Reserved.

Music Sales Corporation for *Cortège* from DEUX MORCEAUX POUR VIOLON ET PIANO by Lili Boulanger. Copyright © 1918, 1981 by G. Schirmer, Inc. (ASCAP). International Copyright Secured. All Rights Reserved. Reprinted by Permission.

Harold Ober Associates, Inc. for *Carol of the Brown King* by Langston Hughes. Reprinted by permission of Harold Ober Associates Incorporated. Copyright © 1958 by Crisis Pub. Co. Copyright renewed 1986 by George Houston Bass.

University of Oklahoma Press for *Señor Don Juan de Pancho* and *Veinte y tres* from HISPANIC FOLK MUSIC OF NEW MEXICO AND THE SOUTHWEST, by John Donald Robb. Copyright © 1980 by the University of Oklahoma Press.

Tom O'Leary for *Treasure Chests* by Tom O'Leary. Copyright © 1981 Tom O'Leary.

Oxford University Press for *Biddy, Biddy (Lost My Gold Ring)* from BROWN GAL IN DE RING by Olive Lewin. Copyright © 1974 Oxford University Press. For *Every Night When the Sun Goes In* from FOLK SONGS OF THE SOUTHERN APPALACHIANS by Cecil Sharp. By permission of Oxford University Press.

Peter Pauper Press for *Ashes my burnt hut* by Hokushi. Copyright © Peter Pauper Press.

Prentice-Hall, Inc. for *Telephone Song* from THE KODALY CONTEXT, p. 236, by Lois Choksy, copyright © 1981. Reprinted by permission of Prentice-Hall Inc., Englewood Cliffs, NJ.

G.P. Putnam's Sons for *The Hungry Waves* by Dorothy Aldis, reprinted by permission of G.P. Putnam's Sons from HERE, THERE AND EVERYWHERE, copyright 1927, 1928, © 1955, 1956 by Dorothy Aldis.

Random House, Inc. for *Alphabet Stew* by Jack Prelutsky from THE RANDOM HOUSE BOOK OF POETRY FOR CHILDREN, selected and introduced by Jack Prelutsky. Copyright © 1983 by Jack Prelutsky. Reprinted by permission of Random House, Inc.

Marian Reiner for *Bicycle Riding* by Sandra Liatsos. Copyright © 1984 by Sandra Liatsos. This poem appeared originally in CRICKET. Reprinted by permission of Marian Reiner for the author. For *Calendar* from A SONG I SANG TO YOU by Myra Cohn Livingston. Copyright © 1984, 1969, 1967, 1965, 1959, 1958 by Myra Cohn Livingston. Reprinted by permission of Marian Reiner for the author.

Rockhaven Music for *Mama Paquita*, a carnival song from Brazil. English lyrics by Merrill Staton © 1986 Rockhaven Music. For *Pat-a-pan*, lyrics by Merrill Staton © 1987 Rockhaven Music.

Scholastic, Inc. for *¡Que llueva!* from ARROZ CON LECHE: POPULAR SONGS AND RHYMES FROM LATIN AMERICA, selected by Lulu Delacre. Copyright © 1989 by Lulu Delacre. Reprinted by permission of Scholastic, Inc.

Charles Scribner's Sons for *Carol* from THE WIND IN THE WILLOWS by Kenneth Grahame. Reprinted with permission of Charles Scribner's Sons, an imprint of Macmillan Publishing Company. Copyright 1933, 1953 Charles Scribner's Sons; copyrights renewed © 1961 Ernest H. Shepard and 1981 Charles Scribner's Sons and Mary Eleanor Jessie Knox.

Kathy B. Sorensen for *Deta, Deta; Oma Rapeti; Tititorea;* and *Wang Ü Ger;* collected and transcribed by Kathy B. Sorensen. Copyright © 1991 Kathy B. Sorensen.

Staff Music Publishing Co., Inc. for *One, Two, Three!*, words and music by Maurice Gardner. Written in the style of a Barbados Work Song. Copyright © 1961 Staff Music Publishing Co., Inc.

Sundance Music for *The Electric Cat*, words and music by Linda Worsley. Copyright © 1988 Sundance Music. *Never Gonna Be Your Valentine*, words and music by Linda Worsley. Copyright © 1986 Sundance Music.

Sweet Pipes Inc. for *Kuma San* from MELODIES FROM THE FAR EAST by Marilyn Copeland Davidson. Copyright © 1990 Sweet Pipes Inc. Used by permission.

Dorothy Brown Thompson for *This Is Halloween* by Dorothy Brown Thompson. Copyright © Dorothy Brown Thompson.

Warner Brothers Publications Inc. for *Autumn to May* by Paul Stookey and Peter Yarrow. © 1962 (Renewed) PEPAMAR MUSIC CORP. All Rights Reserved. Used by Permission. For *Don't Nobody Bring Me No Bad News* by Charlie Smalls. © 1975 WARNER-TAMERLANE PUBLISHING CORP. All Rights Reserved. Used by Permission. For *Rocky Road* by Paul Stookey and Mary Travers. © 1963 (Renewed) PEPAMAR MUSIC CORP. All Rights Reserved. Used by Permission.

ART & PHOTO CREDITS

COVER DESIGN: Designframe Inc., NYC

COVER PHOTOGRAPHY: Jade Albert for MMSD

Cover Set Design by Mark Gagnon
Cello courtesy of Glaesel String Instrument Company/
The Selmer Company Inc.

ILLUSTRATION

Steve Adler, 102-103, 110-111; Doug Aitken, 80-81; Zita Asbaghi, 292-293; George Baquero, 70-71; Ami Blackshear, 154-155; Joe Boddy, 268-269; Doug Bowles, 44-45; Alan Brunettin, 198-199; Kye Carbone, 10-11; Susan Carlson, 18-19; Ben Carter, 200-201; Tony Chen, 274-275; Brian Cody, 180-181, 208-209; Connie Conally, 30-31; Floyd Cooper, 6-7, 120-121; Laura Cornell, 56-57, 192-193; Neverne Covington, 164-165; Jerry Dadds, 209; Stephan Daigle, 300-301; Robert Dale, 22-23; Lisa Desimini, 238-239; David Diaz, 2-3; Julie Downing, 290-291; Brian Dugan, 32-33, 166-167; Andrea Eberbach, 152-153, 167; Clifford Faust, 178-179; Greg Fitzhugh, 62-63; Brad Gaber, 86-87, 244-245; Barbara Garrison, 286-287; Cameron Gerlach, 54-55; Robert Giuliani, 199, 229, 231; Jack Graham, 146-147; Susan Greenstein, 76-77; Lane Gregory, 226-227; John Steven Gurney, 266-267; Abe Gurvin, 206-207; Pam-ela Harrelson, 162-163; Thomas Hart, 256-259; Kevin Hawkes, 158-159; Jennifer Hewitson, 136-137, 166; Celina Hinojosa, 242-243; Catherine Huerta, 200-201; Susan Huls, 278-279, 294-295; Chet Jeziersky, 52-53; Victoria Kann, 132-133; Mark Kaplan, 20-21; Deborah Keats, 224-225; Christa Kieffer, 182-183, 209; Mary King, 202-203; Kathleen Kinkoff, 248-249; Terry Kovalcik, 36-37; Sophia Latto, 232-233; Bryce Lee, 98-99; Fran Lee, 24-25, 41; Richard Leonard, 16-17, 174-175, 208; Steve Madson, 12-13; Michael McCurdy, 88-89; Verlin Miller, 64-65; Yoshi Miyake, 128-129; Christian Musselman, 84-85; Michele Noiset, 134-135, 166, 252-253, 360, 362-369; Yoshikazu Ogino, 274-275; Ed Parker, 8-9, 40-41; Jerry Pavey, 138-139, 166-167; Bob Pepper, 92-93, 104-105, 113, 123-125, 288-289; Evangelia Philippidis, 220-221; Jean Pidgeon, 100-101, 173; Bob Radigan, 30-31, 160-161; Victoria Raymond, 196-197; Lynn Rowe Reed, 74-75; Barbara Reid, 210-211; Glenn Reid, 60-61; Anna Rich, 120-121; Kumiko Robinson, 228-229, 298-299; Kristina Rodanas, 150-151; Sergio Roffo, 50-51; Robert Roper, 90-91, 108-109, 124-127; Doug Roy, 370-379; Joanna Roy, 207; Kristi Schaeppi, 284-285; John Schilling, 270-273; Karen Schmidt, 78-79; Bob Scott, 42-43; Marti Shohet, 276-277; Geo Sipp, 58-59; Joe Spencer, 82-83; Mary Spencer, 108-109; Ken Spengler, 140-141, 167, 216-217; Chris Spollen, 156-157; Michael Steirnagle, 28-29; Susan Swan, 106-107; Peggy Tagel, 14-15, 184-185, 302-303; Julia Talcott, 260-261; Angelo Tillery, 0-1; Winson Trang, 68-69, 144-145; John Turano, 296-297; Jenny Vainisi, 304-305, 308-309; Cornelius van Wright, 282-283; Dale Verzaal, 26-27; Mark Weakley, 48-49; Richard Weber, 116-117, 254-255; Jonathan Wood, 66-67; Susan Hunt Yule, 264-265; Jerry Zimmerman, 34-35.

Tech Art by TCA Graphics, Inc.

PHOTOGRAPHY

All photographs are by the Macmillan/McGraw-Hill School Division (MMSD) except as noted below.

i: instruments, Jim Powell Studio for MMSD. iv-v: instruments, Jim Powell Studio for MMSD. vi: t.l. instruments, Jim Powell Studio for MMSD. **Unit 1** 5: Scott Harvey for MMSD. 7: John Ahearn/Brooke Alexander Gallery NY. 14: Vocal Dynamics Lab/Center for Communications Disorders/Lenox Hill Hospital. 17: Jim Powell Studio for MMSD. 18-19: t. Scott Harvey for MMSD. 20: l. Annie Griffiths Belt/Westlight. 21: l. William Strode/Woodfin Camp & Associates, Inc.; r. Sobel/Klonski/The Image Bank; r. Michal Heron/Woodfin Camp & Associates, Inc. 23: Archiv Fur Kunst Und Geschicte, Berlin/

Photo Researchers, Inc. 31: The Collection of E. Van Hoorick/Superstock. 32: t.l. Archiv Fur Kunst Und Geschicte, Berlin/Photo Researchers, Inc. 38: Diane Padys/FPG International. 40, 41: Bill Waltzer for MMSD. 44-45: Mathers Museum. **Unit 2** 48-49: David Jeffrey/The Image Bank. 58: b.r. Jack Vartoogian. 61: t.r. Museum of Modern Art, NY, Gift of Abby Aldrich Rockefeller. 68: Scott Harvey for MMSD. 71-72: FPG International; b. NASA/FPG International. 72: t.r. Kazunobu Yanagi. 72-73: Patrick Eden/The Image Bank. 73: b.r. Giraudon/Art Resource. 78: Scott Harvey for MMSD. 81: Scott Harvey for MMSD. **Unit 3** 94-95: Adstock Photos/Don B. Stevenson. 96-97: bkgnd. M. Angelo/Westlight. 102: John Running. 103: The Granger Collection. 114-115: George Mars Cassidy/Picture Cube; Alon Reininger/Woodfin Camp & Associates, Inc. 115: Scott Harvey for MMSD. 118: l. The Bettmann Archive. 118-119: b. Roy King. 119: r. Guido Alberto Rossi/The Image Bank. 122: Dennis Brack/Black Star; b., m., t. Scott Harvey for MMSD. 124-125: bkgnd. M. Angelo/Westlight. 125: b. Don B. Stevenson/Adstock. 128: M. Angelo/Westlight; b.l. Owen Seumptewa. 129: Eric Haase. 130: t.l. John Running. 130-131: b.r., m., t.l. John Running. 131: b.r. Courtesy Scohoharie Museum of the Iroquois Indian; m. Courtesy University of South Dakota. **Unit 4** 142-143: Steven Studd/Tony Stone Worldwide. 148: Salzburg Museo di Mozart/Scala/Art Resource. 149: Robert Frerck/Woodfin Camp & Associates, Inc. 169: Bill Waltzer for MMSD. 170-171: m.l. Colonial Williamsburg Foundation. 172: l. Scott Harvey for MMSD. 173: Jim Powell Studio for MMSD. **Unit 5** 174-175: Lance Nelson/Stock Market. 186: t. Susan Wilson. 186-187: b. Jim Powell Studio for MMSD. 190-191: Tony Craddock/Tony Stone Worldwide. 194-195: b. Benjamin Randel/Stock Market. 198: Giraudon/Art Resource. 204: Kunstsammlung Nordrhein-Westfalen, Dusseldorf. 205: Courtesy of Andre Emmerich Gallery, New York. 212: Chad Ehlers/Allstock. 213: Courtesy Aca Galleries, NY. The Estate of Romare Bearden. 214-215: Frank Micelotti. **Unit 6** 219: Courtesy U.S. Committee For Unicef/Scott Harvey for MMSD. 221: b. Marc Romanelli/The Image Bank; m. Doug Armand/Tony Stone Worldwide; t. Bill Ross/Westlight. 227: b. Leo Castelli Gallery; t. The Metropolitan Museum of Art, The Jules Bache Collection, 1940. 228: Christian Steiner/courtesy Sony Classical. 230-231: Jim Powell Studio for MMSD. 232: Chun Y Lai/Esto Photographics. 233: George Pickow. 234-235: Brown Brothers. 236-237: Trevle Wood. 240: Art Resource. 246: Ken Regan/Camera 5; b.m. Jim Powell Studio for MMSD. 247: Jim Powell Studio for MMSD. 250-251: Jim Stratford. 256-257: b. Scott Harvey for MMSD; t.m. Teri Bloom. 257: r. Teri Bloom. 258-259: b. Rafael Wollman/Gamma Liaison; t. Jean Marc Giboux/Gamma Liaison. **Celebrations** 262-263: t. Rafael Macia/Photo Researchers, Inc. 264: Ken Karp for MMSD; Courtesy Harold Leventhal Assoc. 284-285: Ken Karp for MMSD. 296: Walton's Musical Instrument Galleries, Ltd. 304: l. Daemmrich Photos. 304-305: Daemmrich Photos. 308: Czechoslovak News Service/Sovfoto. 309: Dave Bartruff. **Music Library** 356-357: b. Clint Clemens. 357: l., r. Ken Karp for MMSD. 358: b.l. Violin courtesy Sam Ash Music; *Eine Kleine Nachtmusik,* Library of Congress; r. Courtesy Dresden/Meissen Antique Import Corp., New York. 359: l. Photo, Roger-Viollet, Paris.

Macmillan/McGraw-Hill School Division thanks The Selmer Company, Inc., and its Ludwig/Musser Industries and Glaesel String Instrument Company subsidiaries for providing all instruments used in MMSD photographs in this music text-book series, with exceptions as follows. MMSD thanks Yamaha Corporation of America for French horn, euphonium, acoustic and electric guitars, soprano, alto, and bass recorders, piano, and vibraphone; MMB Music Inc., St. Louis, MO, for Studio 49 instruments; Rhythm Band Instruments, Fort Worth, TX, for resonator bells; Courtly Instruments, NY, for soprano and tenor recorder; Elderly Instruments, Lansing, MI, for autoharp, dulcimer, hammered dulcimer, mandolin, Celtic harp, whistles, and Andean flute.

PRONUNCIATION KEY
Simplified International Phonetic Alphabet

VOWELS

ɑ	f<u>a</u>ther	æ	c<u>a</u>t
e	<u>a</u>pe	ɛ	p<u>e</u>t
i	b<u>ee</u>	ι	<u>i</u>t
o	<u>o</u>bey	ɔ	p<u>aw</u>
u	m<u>oo</u>n	ʊ	p<u>u</u>t
ʌ	<u>u</u>p	ə	<u>a</u>go

SPECIAL SOUNDS

β   say *b* without touching lips together; *Spanish* nue<u>v</u>e, ha<u>b</u>a

ç   <u>h</u>ue; *German* i<u>ch</u>

ð   <u>th</u>e, *Spanish* to<u>d</u>o

ṇ   sound <u>n</u> as individual syllable

ö   form [o] with lips and say [e]; *French* ad<u>ieu</u>, *German* sch<u>ö</u>n

œ   form [ɔ] with lips and say [ɛ]; *French* c<u>oeu</u>r, *German* pl<u>ö</u>tzlich

ɾ   flipped r; bu<u>tt</u>er

r̄   rolled r; *Spanish* pe<u>rr</u>o

ǂ   click tongue on the ridge behind teeth; *Zulu* ng<u>c</u>wele

ü   form [u] with lips and say [i]; *French* t<u>u</u>, *German* gr<u>ü</u>n

ü̇   form [ʊ] with lips and say [ι]

x   blow strong current of air with back of tongue up; *German* Ba<u>ch</u>, *Hebrew* <u>H</u>anukkah, *Spanish* ba<u>j</u>o

ʒ   plea<u>s</u>ure

'   glottal stop, as in the exclamation "uh oh!" [ˈʌ ˈo]

~   nasalized vowel, such as French b<u>on</u> [bõ]

˥   end consonants *k*, *p*, and *t* without puff of air, such as s<u>k</u>y (no puff of air after *k*), as opposed to *kite* (puff of air after *k*)

OTHER CONSONANTS PRONOUNCED SIMILAR TO ENGLISH

ch	<u>ch</u>eese	ny	on<u>i</u>on, *Spanish* ni<u>ñ</u>o
g	<u>g</u>o	sh	<u>sh</u>ine
ng	si<u>ng</u>	ts	boa<u>ts</u>

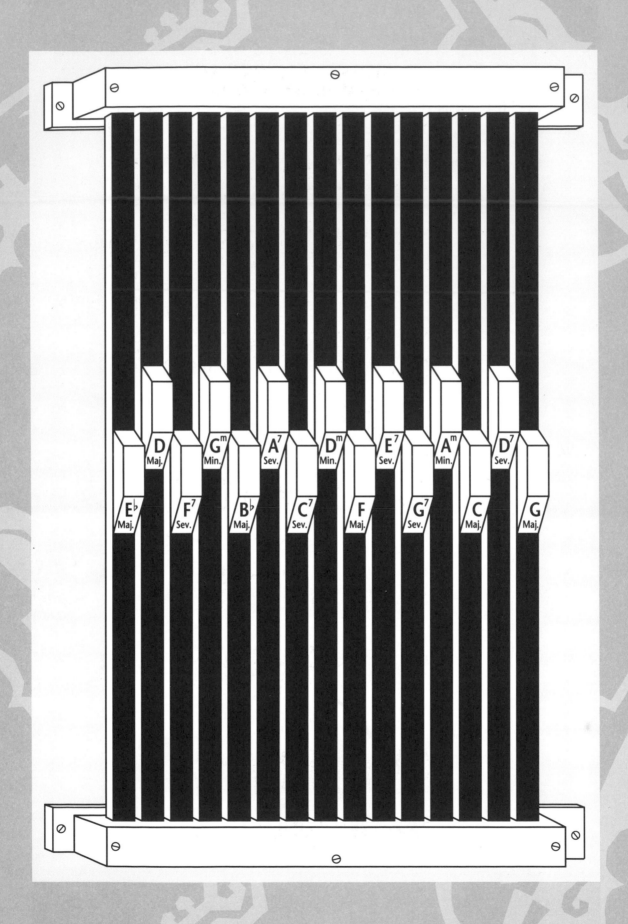